GLOBAL ECONOMIC STUDIES SERIES

THE FINANCIAL CRISIS AND THE EUROPEAN UNION

Global Economic Studies Series

The U.K.'s Rocky Road to Stability
Nicoletta Batini and Edward Nelson (Editor)
2009. ISBN: 978-1-60692-869-1

The Financial Crisis and the European Union
Klaus G. Efenhoff (Editor)
2009. ISBN: 978-1-60741-987-7

GLOBAL ECONOMIC STUDIES SERIES

THE FINANCIAL CRISIS AND THE EUROPEAN UNION

KLAUS G. EFENHOFF
EDITOR

Nova Science Publishers, Inc.
New York

For permission to use material from this book please contact us:
Telephone 631-231-7269; Fax 631-231-8175
Web Site: http://www.novapublishers.com

LIBRARY OF CONGRESS CATALOGING-IN-PUBLICATION DATA
Available upon request
ISBN: 978-1-60741-987-7

Published by Nova Science Publishers, Inc. ✢ New York

CONTENTS

PREFACE

The European Union (EU) is a treaty-based, institutional framework that defines and manages economic and political cooperation among its 27 member states (Austria, Belgium, Bulgaria, Cyprus, the Czech Republic, Denmark, Estonia, Finland, France, Germany, Greece, Hungary, Ireland, Italy, Latvia, Lithuania, Luxembourg, Malta, the Netherlands, Poland, Portugal, Romania, Slovakia, Slovenia, Spain, Sweden and the United Kingdom). The Union is the latest stage in a process of European integration begun after World War II to promote peacc and economic prosperity in Europe. Its founders hoped that by creating communities of shared sovereignty, another war in Europe would be unthinkable. Since the 1950s, this European integration project has expanded to encompass other economic sectors, a customs union, a single market in which goods, people, and capital move freely, a common agricultural policy, and a common currency (the euro). The global financial crisis has hit the EU hard. The latest economic forecasts painted a bleak picture of close to zero growth and risks of contraction for the EU economy in 2009, with unemployment rising by some 2.7 million in the next two years, on the assumption that no corrective action is taken. Quick and decisive action is needed to stop this downward spiral. The interplay of national and EU action can help all Member States weather the worst of the global economic storms and emerge stronger from the crisis.

Chapter 1 - The real test for European governments and institutions comes when faced with the most difficult of circumstances. At such times, they need to show imagination; they need to show determination; and they need to show flexibility. They need to show that they are in tune with the needs of families and communities across the European Union, that they are equal to the task of finding the right response to the sudden downturn in the prospects for growth and jobs in Europe.

Chapter 2 - This chapter describes the European Union (EU), its evolution, governing institutions, trade policy, and efforts to forge common foreign and defense policies. The chapter also addresses the EU-U.S. and EU-NATO relationships, which may be of interest to the second session of the 110th Congress. It will be updated as events warrant. For more information, see CRS Report RS21344, *European Union Enlargement*, by Kristin Archick, and CRS Report RL34381, *European Union-U.S. Trade and Investment Relations: Key Issues*, coordinated by Raymond Ahearn.

Chapter 3 - According to the most recent National Threat Assessment, the global financial crisis and its geopolitical implications pose the primary near-term security concern of the United States. Over the short run, both the EU and the United States are attempting to resolve the financial crisis while stimulating domestic demand to stem the economic downturn. These efforts have born little progress so far as the economic recession and the financial crisis have become reinforcing events, causing EU governments to forge policy responses to both crises. In addition, both the United States and the EU likely will confront the prospect of growing economic and political instability in Eastern Europe and elsewhere over the impact of the economic recession on restive populations. In the long run, the United States and the EU likely will search for a regulatory scheme that provides for greater stability while not inadvertently offering advantages to any one country or group. Throughout the crisis, the European Central Bank and other central banks have assumed a critical role as the primary institutions with the necessary political and economic clout to respond effectively. Within Europe, national governments, private firms, and international organizations have varied in their response to the financial crisis, reflecting differing views over the proper policy course to pursue and the unequal effects of the financial crisis and the economic downturn. Initially, some EU members preferred to address the crisis on a case-by-case basis. As the crisis has persisted, however, leaders have begun looking for a systemic approach that ultimately may affect the drive within Europe toward greater economic integration.

Within the United States, Congress has appropriated funds to help recapitalize financial institutions, and adopted several economic stimulus measures. In addition, Congress likely will be involved in efforts to reshape institutions and frameworks for international cooperation and coordination in financial markets. European governments are also adopting fiscal measures to stimulate their economies and wrestling with failing banks. The financial crisis has demonstrated that financial markets are highly interdependent and that extensive networks link financial markets across national borders, which is pressing EU governments to work together to find a mutually reinforcing solution. Unlike the United States, however, where the federal government can legislate policies that are consistent across all 50 States, the EU process gives each EU member a great deal of discretion to decide how they will regulate and supervise financial markets within their borders. The limits of this system may well be tested as the EU and others search for a regulatory framework that spans a broad number of national markets. Governments that have expended considerable resources utilizing fiscal and monetary policy tools to stabilize the financial system and to provided a boost to their economies may be required to be increasingly more inventive in providing yet more stimulus to their economies and face political unrest in domestic populations. Attention likely will also focus on those governments that are viewed as not expending economic resources commensurate with the size of their economies to stimulate economic growth.

Chapter 4 - This chapter discusses two potential roles the International Monetary Fund (IMF) may have in helping to resolve the current global financial crisis: (1) immediate crisis control through balance of payments lending to emerging market and less-developed countries and (2) increased surveillance of the global economy through better coordination with the international financial regulatory agencies.

Chapter 5 - On November 19, 2008, Iceland and the International Monetary Fund (IMF) finalized an agreement on a $6 billion economic stabilization program supported by a $2.1 billion loan from the IMF. Following the IMF decision, Denmark, Finland, Norway, and Sweden agreed to provide an additional $2.5 billion. Iceland's banking system had collapsed as a culmination of a series of decisions the banks made that left them highly exposed to disruptions in financial markets. The collapse of the banks also raises questions for U.S. leaders and others about supervising banks that operate across national borders, especially as it becomes increasingly difficult to distinguish the limits of domestic financial markets. Such supervision is important for banks that are headquartered in small economies, but operate across national borders. If such banks become so overexposed in foreign markets that a financial disruption threatens the solvency of the banks, the collapse of the banks can overwhelm domestic credit markets and outstrip the ability of the central bank to serve as the lender of last resort.

In: The Financial Crisis and the European Union ISBN: 978-1-60741-987-7
Editor: Klaus G. Efenhoff

Chapter 1

A European Economic Recovery Plan*

Commission of the European Communities

The Time to Act Is Now

The real test for European governments and institutions comes when faced with the most difficult of circumstances. At such times, they need to show imagination; they need to show determination; and they need to show flexibility. They need to show that they are in tune with the needs of families and communities across the European Union, that they are equal to the task of finding the right response to the sudden downturn in the prospects for growth and jobs in Europe.

Europe will above all be judged on results. Since this Commission took office, it has put the spotlight on the European Union's ability to deliver results for its citizens. It has targeted action on areas which will have an impact on Europeans in every corner of the EU. It has championed a partnership approach to work with the key players at every level. It has made clear that the job is not done until the impact is felt on the ground.

The current economic crisis gives another opportunity to show that Europe serves its citizens best when it makes concrete action the touchstone. Europe can make the difference.

---

* This is an edited, reformatted and augmented version of a Commission of the European Communities publication, dated November 26, 2008.

In difficult times, the temptation is to feel powerless. But Europe is not powerless. The levers of government, the instruments of the European Union, the influence of intelligent coordination add up to a potent force to arrest the trend towards a deeper recession. A Europe ready to take swift, bold, ambitious and well-targeted action will be a Europe able to put the brakes on the downturn and begin to turn the tide. We sink or swim together.

The particular contribution of the European Union is its ability to help partners work together. Harnessing Member States' and Community action will add up to a powerful lever for change. It will open the door to using the strengths of each part of Europe to best effect. It will allow us to shape the global response to this global crisis.

A month ago, the Commission took the initiative to set out how decisive and coordinated action could respond to the economic crisis. I am pleased to see that as national governments work to address their own situations, they have been inspired by the common principles agreed for European action. Today the Commission strengthens this platform for joint action with a Plan to contain the scale of the downturn and to stimulate demand and confidence, saving hundreds of thousands of jobs and keeping large and small businesses at work while waiting for growth to return.

The **European Economic Recovery Plan** has two key pillars, and one underlying principle:

- The first pillar is a major injection of purchasing power into the economy, to boost demand and stimulate confidence. The Commission is proposing that, as a matter of urgency, Member States and the EU agree to an immediate budgetary impulse amounting to € 200 billion (1.5% of GDP), to boost demand in full respect of the Stability and Growth Pact.
- The second pillar rests on the need to direct short-term action to reinforce Europe's competitiveness in the long term. The Plan sets out a comprehensive programme to direct action to "smart" investment. Smart investment means investing in the right skills for tomorrow's needs; investing in energy efficiency to create jobs and save energy; investing in clean technologies to boost sectors like construction and automobiles in the low-carbon markets of the future; and investing in infrastructure and inter-connection to promote efficiency and innovation.
- At the same time, the ten Actions for Recovery included in the Plan will help Member States to put the right social and economic levers in place to meet today's challenge: to open up new finance for SMEs, cut administrative burdens and kick-start investment to modernise

infrastructure. It will drive a competitive Europe ready for the low-carbon economy.

- The fundamental principle of this Plan is solidarity and social justice. In times of hardship, our action must be geared to help those most in need. To work to protect jobs through action on social charges. To immediately address the long-term job prospects of those losing their jobs, through the European Globalisation Adjustment Fund and an accelerated European Social Fund. To cut energy costs for the vulnerable through targeted energy efficiency. To address the needs of those who cannot yet use the internet as a tool to connect.

I am convinced that at times of crisis, opportunities open up to accelerate change and to introduce structural reforms to make us succeed in the globalised economy of the future. This is a great opportunity for Europe.

A comprehensive and ambitious recovery plan is now on the table. The quicker we make it happen, the sooner we will bring the help needed to Europeans today.

José Manuel Durão Barroso Brussels, 26th November 2008

1. INTRODUCTION

The global financial crisis has hit the EU hard. A squeeze on credit, falls in house prices and tumbling stock markets are all reinforcing a slump in consumer confidence, consumption and investment. Households are under real pressure. Businesses' order books are down. Sectors dependent on consumer credit – like private construction and the automobile industry – have seen their markets sharply deteriorate in many Member States.

The latest economic forecasts painted a bleak picture of close to zero growth and risks of contraction for the EU economy in 2009, with unemployment rising by some 2.7 million in the next two years, on the assumption that no corrective action is taken. In the weeks since the forecasts came out, economic conditions have deteriorated further:

- Financial market conditions remain fragile, and are likely to be tighter for longer than expected;
- Confidence amongst households and firms has fallen much lower than expected;

- The slowdown has spread to emerging economies with negative effects for European exports.

The euro area and several Member States are already in recession. The risk is that this situation will worsen still further: that investment and consumer purchases will be put off, sparking a vicious cycle of falling demand, downsized business plans, reduced innovation, and job cuts. This could push the EU into a deep and longer-lasting recession: the economy contracting further next year, and unemployment could rise by several million people.

Quick and decisive action is needed to stop this downward spiral. Europe must use all the tools at its disposal. This means Member States and the Union working together, coordinating inside Europe and feeding into a larger global response. In tackling the financial crisis, the Union made sure that the EU level and national action worked together. This was successful in bringing stability at a time of immediate danger. Now Member States should again take advantage of the strengths of the EU – effective coordination, credible frameworks offered by the Stability and Growth Pact and the Lisbon Strategy, as well as the benefits of scale offered by the euro and the largest single market in the world. The interplay of national and EU action can help all Member States weather the worst of the global economic storms and emerge stronger from the crisis.

The euro, in particular, has proved to be an invaluable asset for the EU economies and an essential element of stability. Supported by the strong role played by the independent European Central Bank, the euro protects against destabilising exchange rate movements, which would have greatly complicated the national responses to the crisis.

A month ago, the Commission took the initiative to outline its plans for dealing with the financial crisis, addressing the difficulties of the wider economy and making Europe a key player in the global response to the financial crisis[1]. In early November, the EU's Heads of State and Government agreed on the need for a coordinated response and asked the Commission to make proposals for discussion at their December meeting.

A European Economic Recovery Plan

This **European Economic Recovery Plan** is the Commission's response to the current economic situation. Given the scale of the crisis we are facing, the EU needs a co-ordinated approach, big enough and ambitious enough to restore consumer and business confidence. It needs to bring together all the policy levers available at EU and national level. Most of the economic policy levers, and in particular those which can stimulate consumer demand in the short term, are in the hands of the Member States. Member States have very different starting points in terms of fiscal room for manoeuvre. But that makes effective coordination all the more important.

All Member States will need to take action to deal with the crisis. Properly coordinated, national efforts can target different goals in parallel. They can cushion the blow of recession in the short term. But they can also promote the structural reforms needed to help the EU emerge stronger from the crisis, without undermining longer term fiscal sustainability. For this reason, this Recovery Plan puts particular emphasis on innovation and greening of EU investment. The EU level can act as a catalyst for such "smart action," combining EU policies and funds to help Member States maintain or pull forward investments which will create jobs, boost demand, and strengthen Europe's capacity to benefit from globalisation.

The strategic aims of the Recovery Plan are to:

- Swiftly stimulate demand and boost consumer confidence;
- Lessen the human cost of the economic downturn and its impact on the most vulnerable. Many workers and their families are or will be hit by the crisis. Action can be taken to help stem the loss of jobs; and then to help people return rapidly to the labour market, rather than face long-term unemployment;
- Help Europe to prepare to take advantage when growth returns so that the European economy is in tune with the demands of competitiveness and the needs of the future, as outlined in the Lisbon Strategy for Growth and Jobs. That means pursuing the necessary structural reforms, supporting innovation, and building a knowledge economy;
- Speed up the shift towards a low carbon economy. This will leave Europe well placed to apply its strategy for limiting climate change and promoting energy security: a strategy which will encourage new technologies, create new 'green-collar' jobs and open up new opportunities in fast growing world markets, will keep energy bills for citizens and businesses in check, and will reduce Europe's dependence on foreign energy.

In pursuing these aims, the European Economic Recovery Plan is designed to:

- Exploit synergies and avoid negative spill-over effects through co-ordinated action;
- Draw on all available policy levers, fiscal policies, structural and financial market reforms and external action;
- Ensure full coherence between immediate actions and the EU's medium- to longer term objectives;
- Take full account of the global nature of the problem and shape the EU's contribution to international responses.

This European Economic Recovery Plan proposes a counter-cyclical macro-economic response to the crisis in the form of an ambitious set of actions to support the real economy. The aim is to avoid a deep recession. The Plan is anchored in the Stability and Growth Pact and the Lisbon Strategy for Growth and Jobs. It consists of:

- An immediate budgetary impulse amounting to € 200 bn (1.5% of EU GDP), made up of a budgetary expansion by Member States of € 170 bn (around 1.2% of EU GDP), and EU funding in support of immediate actions of the order of € 30 bn (around 0.3 % of EU GDP);
- And a number of priority actions, grounded in the Lisbon Strategy, and designed at the same time to adapt our economies to long-term challenges, continuing to implement structural reforms aimed at raising potential growth.

2. Supporting the Real Economy and Boosting Confidence

As the economies of all Member States are highly integrated, sharing one single market and many common policies, any response must combine monetary and credit aspects, budgetary policy, and actions in the Lisbon strategy for growth and jobs.

2.1. Monetary and Credit Conditions

2.1.1. The Role of the European Central Bank and Other Central Banks

In the current juncture, monetary policy has a crucial role to play. In the light of reduced inflationary expectation over the medium-term, the European Central Bank (ECB) for the euro area, along with other EU central banks, has already cut interest rates. The ECB has signalled that there is scope for further reductions. The ECB has already demonstrated its importance in stabilising markets by lending to banks and contributing to liquidity.

2.1.2. The Role of Banks

At the root of the problems in the real economy lies the instability in the financial markets. A reliable and efficient financial sector is a pre-requisite for a healthy, growing economy. Stabilising the banking system is therefore the first step towards halting the downturn and promoting a swift and sustainable recovery. The EU must maintain this common drive to rebuild stability and confidence in the still-fragile financial sector and create the conditions for a sustained economic recovery. The crisis has shown risks in the current governance of financial markets which have or could become real and systemic in times of serious turbulence. The pace of reform will be maintained in the coming months to restore stability and protect the interests of European citizens and business.

But it is now crucial that banks resume their normal role of providing liquidity and supporting investment in the real economy. Member States should use the major financial support provided to the banking sector to encourage a return to normal lending activities and to ensure that central interest rate cuts are passed on to borrowers. The Commission will continue to monitor the economic and competition impacts of measures taken to support the banking sector.

2.1.3. The Role of the European Investment Bank and the European Bank for Reconstruction and Development

The current crisis requires reinforced interventions from the European Investment Bank (EIB) group. The EIB will increase its yearly interventions in the EU by some €15 billion for the next two years. As this increased activity will take the form of loans, equity, guarantees and risk-sharing financing, it will also generate a positive leverage of additional investment from private sources. In total, this package proposed by EIB will help mobilise complementary private resources to support additional investments over the next two years. To enable the EIB to increase its financing activities, Member States should decide before the end of the year to incorporate EIB's reserves to reinforce its capital base in the order of € 60 bn, which will provide a highly visible political signal to the markets and which will significantly increase the Bank's lending capacity. The European Bank for Reconstruction and Development (EBRD) is also expected to add €500 million per year to its present level of financing in the new Member States.

2.2. Budgetary Policy

Restoring confidence will depend on Europe's ability to boost demand by making use of budgetary policy within the flexibility offered by the revised Stability and Growth Pact. In the current circumstances, budgetary policy has an even more important role to play in stabilising economies and sustaining demand.

Only through a significant stimulus package can Europe counter the expected downward trend in demand, with its negative knock-on effects on investments and employment. Therefore, the Commission proposes that Member States agree a co-ordinated budgetary stimulus package which should be timely, targeted and temporary, to be implemented immediately.

In the context of national budgets for 2009, this co-ordinated budgetary impulse should be € 170 bn, which represents 1.2% of the Union's GDP, in order to produce a substantive positive and rapid impact on the European economy and on employment, in addition to the role of the automatic stabilisers. Expenditures and/or reductions in taxation included in the budgetary impulse should be consistent with the flexibility offered by the Stability and Growth Pact and reinforce the structural reforms of the Lisbon Strategy. This budgetary stimulus should be temporary. Member States should commit to reverse the budgetary deterioration and return to the aims set out in the medium term objectives.

To maximise its impact, the budgetary stimulus should take account of the starting positions of each Member State. It is clear that not all Member States are in the same position. Those that took advantage of the good times to achieve more sustainable public finance positions and improve their competitive positions have more room for manoeuvre now. For those Member States, in particular outside the euro area, which are facing significant external and internal imbalances, budgetary policy should essentially aim at correcting such imbalances.

This budgetary stimulus must be well designed and be based on the following principles:

1. It should be timely, temporary, targeted, and co-ordinated

National budgetary stimulus packages should be:

- timely so that they quickly support economic activity during the period of low demand, as delays in implementation could mean that the fiscal impulse only comes when the recovery is underway;
- temporary so as to avoid a permanent deterioration in budgetary positions which would undermine sustainability and eventually require financing through sustained future tax increases;
- targeted towards the source of the economic challenge (increasing unemployment, credit constrained firms/households, etc. and supporting structural reforms) as this maximises the stabilisation impact of limited budgetary resources;
- co-ordinated so that they multiply the positive impact and ensure long term budgetary sustainability.

2. It should mix revenue and expenditure instruments.

In general, discretionary public spending is considered to have a stronger positive impact on demand in the short-run compared with tax cuts. This is because some consumers may prefer to save rather than spend, unless the tax cuts are limited in time. Taking the different situations of Member States into account the following measures could be considered [2]:

- Public expenditure has an impact on demand in the short-term. Measures that can be introduced quickly and targeted at households which are especially hard hit by the slowdown are likely to feed through almost directly to consumption, e.g., temporarily increased transfers to the unemployed or low income households, or a temporary lengthening of the duration of unemployment benefit. This can also be done through frontloading public investment in projects which could benefit SMEs and could support long-term public policy goals such as improving infrastructure endowments or tackling climate change;
- Guarantees and loan subsidies to compensate for the unusually high current risk premium can be particularly effective in an environment where credit is generally constrained. They can help bridge a lack of short-term of working capital which is currently a problem for many companies;
- Well designed financial incentives for speeding up the adaptation of our economies to long-term challenges such as climate change, including for example incentives for energy efficiency;

- Lower taxes and social contributions: lower social contributions paid by employers can have a positive impact on job retention and creation while lower taxation of labour income can support purchasing power in particular for low wage earners;
- Temporary reductions in the level of the standard rate of VAT can be introduced quickly and might provide a fiscal impulse to support consumption.

3. It should be conducted within the Stability and Growth Pact.

Budgetary policy should be conducted within the Stability and Growth Pact, so as to provide a common and credible framework for policy. The 2005 revision of the Pact allows better account to be taken of cyclical conditions while strengthening medium and long-term fiscal discipline. The resulting framework is more demanding in good times, it affords more flexibility in bad times. Extraordinary circumstances combining a financial crisis and a recession justify a co-ordinated budgetary expansion in the EU. It may lead some Member States to breach the 3% GDP deficit reference value. For Member States considered to be in an excessive deficit, corrective action will have to be taken in time frames consistent with the recovery of the economy. This is fully consistent with the procedures of the Stability and Growth Pact which guarantee that the excessive deficit will be corrected in due time, ensuring long-term sustainability of the budgetary positions.

The Stability and Growth Pact will therefore be applied judiciously ensuring credible medium-term fiscal policy strategies. Member States putting in place counter-cyclical measures should submit an updated Stability or Convergence Programme by the end of December 2008. This update should spell out the measures that will be put in place to reverse the fiscal deterioration and ensure long-term sustainability. The Commission will then assess the budgetary impulse measures and stability and convergence programmes based on updated forecasts and will provide guidance on the appropriate stance, relying on the following objectives:

- ensuring the reversibility of measures increasing deficits in the short term;
- improving budgetary policy-making in the medium-term, through a strengthening of the national budgetary rules and frameworks;
- ensuring long-term sustainability of public finances, in particular through reforms curbing the rise in age-related expenditure.

4. It should be accompanied by structural reforms that support demand and promote resilience.

While the most immediate impact on growth and jobs in the short run needs to come from a monetary and fiscal stimulus, a comprehensive recovery plan also needs to encompass an ambitious **structural reform agenda** tailored to the needs of individual Member States, and designed to equip them to emerge stronger from the crisis. In part, this is because some structural reforms can also contribute to bolstering aggregate demand in the short term. Moreover, structural reforms are necessary to address some of the underlying root causes of the present crisis, as well as to strengthen the economy's adjustment capacity needed for a rapid recovery.

A resilient, flexible economy helps mitigate the adverse impact of an economic crisis. The Lisbon Strategy has already strengthened the European economic fundamentals. Appropriately tailored, Lisbon strategy structural reforms could be an appropriate short-term policy response to the crisis as they strengthen economic resilience and flexibility. Member States should consider the following measures:

- *Supporting consumer purchasing power through improved market functioning:* policies that improve the functioning of key markets can help sustain demand by helping bring down prices, thus supporting the purchasing power of households;
- *Addressing immediate competitiveness problems.* In Member States with inflation and competitiveness problems measures need to be taken urgently that reinforce the link between the wage setting mechanism and productivity developments;
- *Supporting employment and facilitating labour market transitions*: today's prime labour market challenge is to avoid wasteful labour shedding by industries temporarily affected by short-term demand disturbances. To that end, more flexibility in working time arrangements or enhanced employment services could help;
- *Reducing regulatory and administrative burdens on businesses.* Such reforms help increase productivity, and strengthen competitiveness. Measures that can be implemented rapidly include continuing efforts to reduce the time to start up a business.

2.3. Actions in the Four Priority Areas of the Lisbon Strategy

In order to produce maximum benefits and achieve the Recovery Plan's aims of protecting people and preventing the crisis from deflecting attention from the EU's longer-term interests and the need to invest in its future, there should be a close connection between the fiscal stimulus and actions in the four priority areas of the Lisbon Strategy (people, business, infrastructure and energy, research and innovation), as outlined in this section. In order to achieve this, as part of its annual Lisbon package, the Commission will issue individual reports for each Member State on 16 December 2008 which will include proposals for recommendations.

A smart combination of EU policies and funds can act as a catalyst for key investments taking the EU in the direction of future sustainable prosperity. It is equally important to provide for stable foreseeable framework conditions to boost confidence, facilitate investment and to work for least cost solutions to common problems. Some of the actions proposed in this section are designed to frontload EU funding directly to contribute to the fiscal stimulus and assist Member States with the implementation of their policies. Others are intended to improve the framework conditions for future investments, reduce administrative burdens and speed up innovation. Overall, the actions form an integrated package: their budgetary implications should take into account the principles set out in the previous section.

2.3.1. Protecting Employment and Promoting Entrepreneurship

The top priority must be to protect Europe's citizens from the worst effects of the financial crisis. They are the first to be hit whether as workers, households, or as entrepreneurs. In addressing the employment and social impact of the financial crisis, Member States should actively involve the social partners.

a) People

The implementation of active inclusion and integrated flexicurity policies, focused on activation measures, re-training and skills upgrading, are essential to promote employability, ensure rapid re-integration into the labour market of workers who have been made redundant and avoid long term unemployment. Within this context, adequate social protection that provides incentives to work whilst preserving purchasing power will also be important.

b) Business

Sufficient and affordable access to finance is a pre-condition for investment, growth and job creation by the private sector. Member States need to use the leverage they have through the provision of major financial support to the banking sector to ensure that banks resume their normal lending activities. To support small businesses and entrepreneurship, the EU and Member States must take urgent steps to substantially reduce administrative burdens for SMEs and micro-enterprises, in particular by fast-tracking the corresponding Commission's proposals. To this end, the European Small Business Act should also be implemented as soon as possible.

1. Launch a major European employment support initiative.

a) The Commission is proposing to simplify criteria for European Social Fund (ESF) support and step up advance payments from early 2009, so that Member States have earlier access to up to € 1.8 bn in order to:

- Within flexicurity strategies, rapidly reinforce activation schemes, in particular for the low-skilled, involving personalised counselling, intensive (re-)training and upskilling of workers, apprenticeships, subsidised employment as well as grants for self-employment, business start-up's and
- Refocus their programmes to concentrate support on the most vulnerable, and where necessary opt for full Community financing of projects during this period;
- Improve the monitoring and matching of skills development and upgrading with existing and anticipated job vacancies; this will be implemented in close cooperation with social partners, public employment services and universities;

Working with Member States, the Commission proposes to re-programme ESF expenditure to ensure that immediate priorities are met.

those who are made redundant or to keep in the labour market skilled workers who will be needed once the economy starts to recover. The Commission will review the budgetary means available for the Fund in the light of the implementation of the revised rules.

b) The Commission will also propose to revise the rules of the European Globalisation Adjustment Fund so that it can intervene more rapidly in key sectors, either to co- finance training and job placements for

2. Create demand for labour.

- Member States should consider reducing employers' social charges on lower incomes to promote the employability of lower skilled workers. Member States should also consider the introduction of innovative solutions (e.g., service cheques for household and child care, temporary hiring subsidies for vulnerable groups), which have already been successfully pioneered in parts of the Union;
- The Council should adopt, before the 2009 Spring European Council, the proposed directive to make permanent reduced VAT rates for labour-intensive services.

The EU's state aid rules offer Member States a wide range of possibilities for providing financial support to companies, regions and workers/the unemployed and to stimulate demand. At the same time these rules guarantee a level playing field, ensuring that state aids are used to support EU objectives such as R&D, innovation, ICT, transport and energy efficiency, and not to unduly distort competition by favouring particular companies or sectors. In the current exceptional circumstances, access to finance is a major business concern and the Commission will develop temporary guidelines allowing state support for loans (see below).

3. Enhance access to financing for business.

- The EIB has put together a package of € 30 bn for loans to SME's, an increase by € 10 billion over its usual lending in this sector;
- The EIB will also reinforce by € 1 bn a year its lending to mid-sized corporations, a key sector of the EU economy. Furthermore, an additional € 1 billion will be conferred by the EIB to the EIF for a mezzanine finance facility;

The Commission will put in place a simplification package, notably to speed up its State aid decision-making. Any state aid should be channelled through horizontal schemes designed to promote the Lisbon objectives, notably research, innovation, training, environmental protection and in particular clean technologies, transport and energy efficiency. The Commission will temporarily authorise Member States to ease access to finance for companies through subsidised guarantees and loan subsidies for investments in products going beyond EU environmental standards [3].

addition, Member States should re-programme their structural funds
erational programmes to devote a greater share to energy-efficiency
vestments, including where they fund social housing. To widen
ssibilities, the Commission is proposing an amendment to the
ructural Funds Regulations to support this move and stresses the need
r early adoption of the amendments;
he Commission will work with the EIB and a number of national
evelopment banks to launch a 2020 fund for energy, climate change and
frastructure to fund equity and quasi-equity projects;
he Commission calls on Member States and industry urgently to
evelop innovative financing models, for example, where refurbishments
re financed through repayments, based on savings made on energy bills,
ver several years.

romote the rapid take-up of "green products."

The Commission will propose reduced VAT rates for green products and services, aimed at improving in particular energy efficiency of buildings. It encourages Member States to provide further incentives to consumers to stimulate demand for environmentally-friendly products;
In addition, Member States should rapidly implement environmental performance requirements for external power supplies, stand-by and off mode electric power consumption, set top boxes and fluorescent lamps;
The Commission will urgently draw up measures for other products which offer very high potential for energy savings such as televisions, domestic lighting, refrigerators and freezers, washing machines, boilers and air-conditioners.

rch and Innovation

financial crisis and the subsequent squeeze on financial resources, both
d private, may tempt some to delay, or substantially cut, planned R&D
ation investments, as has happened in the past when Europe was hit by a
n. With hindsight, such decisions amounted to a major capital and
ge destruction with very negative effects for Europe's growth and
ent prospects in the medium to longer-term. However, there have also
amples of countries, both inside and outside Europe, which had the
t to increase R&D and education expenditure in difficult economic times
h they laid the basis for their strong position in innovation.

4. Reduce administrative burdens and promote entrepreneurship.

Building on the Small Business Act, and in order significantly reduce administrative burdens on business, promote their cash flow and help more people to become entrepreneurs, the EU and Member States should:

- Ensure that starting up a business anywhere in the EU can be done within three days at zero costs and that formalities for the hiring of the first employee can be fulfilled via a single access point;
- Remove the requirement on micro-enterprises to prepare annual accounts (the estimated savings for these companies are € 7bn per year) and limit the capital requirements of the European private company to one euro;
- Accelerate the adoption of the European private company statute proposal so that from early 2009 it can facilitate cross border business activities of SMEs and to allow them to work under a single set of corporate rules across the EU;
- Ensure that public authorities pay invoices, including to SMEs, for supplies and services within one month to ease liquidity constraints and accept e-invoicing as equivalent to paper invoicing (this could deliver cost reductions of up to 18 € Bn); any arrears owed by public bodies should also be settled;
- Reduce by up to 75% the fees for patent applications and maintenance and halve the costs for an EU trademark.

2.3.2. Continuing to Invest in the Future

We are witnessing the beginning of a major structural shift towards a low carbon economy. This provides the EU with an opportunity that will create new businesses, new industries and millions of new well-paying jobs. All sectors must participate: for example, the recent decision on the CAP health check commits €3 Bn for climate-friendly investments in rural development. This is where short-term action can bring immediate as well as lasting benefits to the Union. To accelerate investments, the Commission will clarify the legal framework for partnerships between the public and private sector aiming at carrying out major infrastructure and research investments, in order to facilitate this mixed mode of financing.

c) Infrastructure and Energy

The key to maximising benefits and minimising costs is to target opportunities to boost energy efficiency, for example, of buildings, lighting, cooling and heating systems, and of other technologies like vehicles and machinery. Major positive effects for households and businesses can be harvested in the short term.

At the same time, Europe needs to accelerate its investments in infrastructure, particularly in the environmentally-friendly transport-modes which are part of the Trans-European Networks (TENs), high-speed ICT networks, energy interconnections, and pan-European research infrastructures. Speeding up infrastructure investments will not only cushion the blow to the construction sector, which is slowing down sharply in most Member States, it will also enhance Europe's longer-term sustainable growth-potential. Particularly in the energy sector a number of high profile trans-European projects would help to increase the EU's energy security and integrate more Member States into the European electricity grid.

5. Step up investments to modernise Europe's infrastructure.

- For at least the next two years, the EU budget is unlikely to spend the full amount set out in the financial framework. Therefore, for 2009 and 2010, the Commission proposes to mobilise an additional € 5 bn for trans-European energy interconnections and broadband infrastructure projects. To make this happen, Council and Parliament will need to agree to revise the financial framework, while remaining within the limits of the current budget;
- With a financial envelope of over € 347 bn for 2007-2013, cohesion policy provides considerable support to public investment by Member States and regions. However, there is a risk that pressure on national budgets will slow down the rate of planned investment. To give an immediate boost to the economy, the implementation of the structural funds should be accelerated. To this end:
- The Commission will propose to increase its pre-financing of programmes to make up to € 4.5 bn available earlier in 2009;
- Member States should use the available flexibility to frontload the financing of projects by enhancing the part financed by the Community;

- The Commission will propose a number
bring forward the implementation of
facilitate the use of financial engineering
of advances paid to the beneficiaries and
eligible expenditure on a flat rate basis for

The Commission underlines the need for early

- By the end of March 2009 the Commissio
call for proposals for trans-European trans
this money would lead to construction begi
This will bring forward existing funds that
by the mid-term review of the multi- annual
- In parallel, the EIB will significantly incr
change, energy security and infrastructure in
year, while also accelerating the implemen
financial instruments jointly developed wi
Risk Sharing Finance Facility to support R&
Instrument for TEN-T projects to stimulate
private sector;
- The EBRD will more than double its efforts f
change mitigation and financing for
infrastructure services. This could lead throug
sector financing to € 5 bn investments.

6. Improve energy efficiency in buildings.

Acting together, Member States and EU Instit
measures to improve the energy efficiency of the
buildings and promote rapid take up of 'green' products

- Member States should set demanding targets
buildings and both private and social housing
energy-efficiency standards and make them subj
on a regular basis. To facilitate reaching their
States should consider introducing a reduction o
performing buildings. The Commission has just
major upgrading in the energy efficiency of bu
Council and Parliament to give priority to their ac

7.

d) Rese

The
public
and edu
downtu
knowle
employ
been e
foresig
by whi

8. Increase investment in R&D , Innovation and Education.

Member States and the private sector should increase planned investments in education and R&D (consistent with their national R&D targets) to stimulate growth and productivity. They should also consider ways to increase private sector R&D investments, for example, by providing fiscal incentives, grants and/or subsidies. Member States should maintain investments to increase the quality of education.

9. Developing clean technologies for cars and construction.

To support innovation in manufacturing, in particular in the construction industry and the automobile sector which have recently seen demand plummet as a result of the crisis and which also face significant challenges in the transition to the green economy, the Commission proposes to launch 3 major partnerships between the public and private sectors:

- In the automobile sector, a 'European green cars initiative', involving research on a broad range of technologies and smart energy infrastructures essential to achieve a breakthrough in the use of renewable and non-polluting energy sources, safety and traffic fluidity. The partnership would be funded by the Community, the EIB, industry and Member States' contributions with a combined envelope of at least € 5 bn. In this context, the EIB would provide cost-based loans to car producers and suppliers to finance innovation, in particular in technologies improving the safety and the environmental performance of cars, e.g. electric vehicles. Demand side measures such as a reduction by Member States of their registration and circulation taxes for lower emission cars, as well as efforts to scrap old cars, should be integrated into the initiative. In addition, the Commission will support the development of a procurement network of regional and local authorities to pool demand for clean buses and other vehicles and speed up the implementation of the CARS21 initiative;

- In the construction sector, a 'European energy-efficient buildings' initiative, to promote green technologies and the development of energy-efficient systems and materials in new and renovated buildings with a view to reducing radically their energy consumption and CO2 emissions[5]. The initiative should have an important regulatory and standardisation component and would involve a procurement network of regional and local authorities. The estimated envelope for this partnership is € 1bn. The initiative would be backed by specific actions proposed under actions 5 and 6 on infrastructure and energy-efficiency;
- To increase the use of technology in manufacturing, "a factories of the future initiative": The objective is to help EU manufacturers across sectors, in particular SMEs, to adapt to global competitive pressures by increasing the technological base of EU manufacturing through the development and integration the enabling technologies of the future, such as engineering technologies for adaptable machines and industrial processes, ICT, and advanced materials. The estimated envelope for this action is € 1.2 bn.

10. High-speed Internet for all

High-speed Internet connections promote rapid technology diffusion, which in turn creates demand for innovative products and services. Equipping Europe with this modern infrastructure is as important as building the railways in the nineteenth century. To boost Europe's lead in fixed and wireless communications and accelerate the development of high value-added services, the Commission and Member States should work with stakeholders to develop a broadband strategy to accelerate the up-grading and extension of networks. The strategy will be supported by public funds in order to provide broadband access to under-served and high cost areas where the market cannot deliver. The aim should be to reach 100% coverage of high speed internet by 2010. In addition, and also with a view to upgrading the performance of existing networks, Member States should promote competitive investments in fibre networks and endorse the Commission's proposals to free up spectrum for wireless broadband. Using the funding mentioned in action 5 above, the Commission will channel an additional € 1 bn to these network investments in 2009/10.

3. Working towards Global Solutions

The challenges the EU is now facing are part of the global macro economic challenges highlighted by the recent Summit on Financial Markets and the World Economy in Washington. This European Economic Recovery Plan will form part of the EU's contribution to closer international macro economic co-operation, including with emerging countries, designed to restore growth, avoid negative spillovers and support developing countries. The EU has benefited greatly in recent decades from increased cross-border capital and trade flows with developed countries and increasingly also with emerging economies. The financial crisis has shown just how interdependent the world has become. The scale and speed at which a loss of confidence in one part of the world soon affected financial markets and spilt over to real economies worldwide is rightly a matter of concern. In today's world, a shock to one systemically important financial market is a global problem and has to be treated accordingly. So a key part of any co-ordinated EU response to the economic downturn will have to come through greater engagement with our international partners, and with international organisations, working together to tackle challenges at home and abroad, including in developing countries which will be among those hardest hit.

Keeping World Trade Moving

Europe's recovery depends on our companies' ability to make best use of the possibilities that global markets offer. Europe's return to solid growth will also depend on its capacity to export. Keeping trade links and investment opportunities open is also the best means to limit the global impact of the crisis, since global recovery will depend crucially on the sustainable economic performance of emerging and developing economies.

We must therefore maintain our commitment to open markets across the globe, keeping our own market as open as possible and insisting that third countries do the same, in particular by ensuring compliance with WTO rules. To reach this objective Europe should take renewed action to:

- Reach early agreement on a global trade deal in the WTO Doha Round. Following the renewed commitment made at the 15 November Washington Summit, the Commission has immediately stepped up efforts with key WTO partners to reach an agreement on modalities by the end of the year. A successful Round will send a strong short-term signal of confidence in the new global economic order. Over time it will bring consumers and businesses all over the world benefits in terms of lower prices, by cutting remaining high tariffs in key partner markets;

- Continue to support the economic and social consolidation of the candidate countries and the Western Balkans in the mutual interest of the EU and the region. To this end the Commission will put in place a € 120 million "Crisis Response Package" leveraging an amount of € 500 million in loans from International Financial Institutions;
- Create a network of deep and comprehensive free trade agreements in its neighbourhood as a step towards a more integrated regional market. Working through its neighbourhood policy, the EU can build on the Union for the Mediterranean and its plans for a new Eastern Partnership;
- Step up efforts to secure new and ambitious Free Trade Agreements with other trade partners;
- Build a close working relationship with the new US administration, including through the Transatlantic Economic Council. More effective regulatory cooperation could also be pursued with other key industrialised countries, such as Canada and Japan;
- Continue dialogues with key bilateral partners such as China, India, Brazil and Russia and use them to address public procurement, competition and intellectual property issues.

Tackling Climate change

The crisis is occurring on the eve of a major structural shift towards the low carbon economy. The goal of fighting climate change can be combined with major new economic opportunities to develop new technologies and create jobs and enhance energy security.

Agreement in the December European Council and with the European Parliament on the EU's internal climate change strategy will strengthen the leading role the EU must seek to play in securing an ambitious international agreement on climate change at the UNFCCC conference in Copenhagen at the end of 2009.

Supporting Developing Countries

The current crisis will further add to existing pressures on developing countries, which are often least well positioned to cope. So it is all the more important that the EU, and others, maintain their commitments to achieving the Millennium Development Goals (MDG). It may also be necessary for developed countries and regions, like the EU, to come up with new, flexible and innovative instruments to help developing countries face the rapid impact of the crisis such as the EU's recent food aid facility.

Continuing to help emerging and developing countries on the path to sustainable growth is particularly relevant in the run up to the International Conference on Financing for Development, which will take place in Doha from 29 November – 2 December. At this meeting, the EU – which in 2007 continued to be the largest donor of Overseas Development Assistance (ODA) - will reaffirm its commitment to arriving at ODA target levels of 0.56% of GNP by 2010 and 0.7% by 2015. It will also invite other donors to continue to work towards these goals.

Supporting sustainable development, *inter alia* through delivering on ODA targets and MDG goals, but also through addressing overall governance challenges, is all the more important in times of economic crisis. Sharing the benefits of sustainable growth, tackling climate change, energy and food security and good governance, are interlinked challenges, where international financial institutions, like other international bodies, also have an important role to play.

4. CONCLUSIONS

It is clear that the EU faces a difficult time in the coming months as the effects of the world and European economic slow down puts pressure on jobs and demand. But, acting together, Member States and European Institutions can take action to restore consumer and business confidence, to restart lending and stimulate investment in our economies, creating jobs and helping the unemployed to find new jobs. **The European Economic Recovery Plan** set out in this Communication is designed to create a basis for rapid agreement between Member States to get Europe's economy moving again.

The European Commission calls on the European Parliament to lend its full support to this European Economic Recovery Plan.

It calls on Heads of State and Government, at their meeting on 11 and 12 December 2008, to:

1. Endorse this European Economic Recovery Plan;
2. Request the European Commission and the Council to work together to ensure that combined national and EU level measures amount to at least 1.5% of GDP;
3. Ensure that updated Stability and Convergence Programmes including the national impulse measures, are assessed in accordance with the procedures laid down in the Stability and Growth Pact, while making use of the flexibility it offers;
4. Endorse the 10 actions outlined in the European Economic Recovery Plan; urge the Council and Parliament to accelerate any legislative activity needed to implement these measures;
5. Agree, on the basis of a Commission contribution before the 2009 Spring European Council assessing progress made with the implementation of the Plan, to identify any further measures necessary at EU and Member State level to stimulate the recovery;
6. Continue to work closely with international partners to implement global solutions to strengthen global governance and promote the economic recovery.

References

[1] **Communication of 29 October - COM(2008) 706.**

[2] The general recommendations and the specific actions related to the priority areas set out in this document are subject to compliance with internal market and competition rules, notably for State aid.

[3] This will be done by raising the current €1.5 M safe harbour threshold for risk capital to € 2.5M, and by allowing, subject to certain conditions and maximum amounts, (a) to grant aid for guarantees for loans for certain companies having difficulties to obtain loans ; and (b) to grant aid of up to 50% (for SMEs and 25% (for large companies) of the Reference Rate, for loans for investments in the manufacture of products complying earlier with, or going beyond, new Community standards which increase the level of environmental protection and are not yet in force.

[4] COM(2008) 755, 13.11.2008.

[5] Buildings currently account for 40% of energy consumption.

In: The Financial Crisis and the European Union ISBN: 978-1-60741-987-7
Editor: Klaus G. Efenhoff

Chapter 2

THE EUROPEAN UNION: QUESTIONS AND ANSWERS*

Kristin Archick

ABSTRACT

This chapter describes the European Union (EU), its evolution, governing institutions, trade policy, and efforts to forge common foreign and defense policies. The chapter also addresses the EU-U.S. and EU-NATO relationships, which may be of interest to the second session of the 110th Congress. For more information, see CRS Report RS21344, *European Union Enlargement*, by Kristin Archick, and CRS Report RL34381, *European Union-U.S. Trade and Investment Relations: Key Issues*, coordinated by Raymond Ahearn.

WHAT IS THE EU?

The EU is a treaty-based, institutional framework that defines and manages economic and political cooperation among its 27 member states (Austria, Belgium, Bulgaria, Cyprus, the Czech Republic, Denmark, Estonia, Finland, France, Germany, Greece, Hungary, Ireland, Italy, Latvia, Lithuania, Luxembourg, Malta, the Netherlands, Poland, Portugal, Romania, Slovakia,

* This is an edited, reformatted and augmented version of a CRS Report RS21372, dated July 3, 2008.

Slovenia, Spain, Sweden, and the United Kingdom). The Union is the latest stage in a process of European integration begun after World War II to promote peace and economic prosperity in Europe. Its founders hoped that by creating communities of shared sovereignty — initially in areas of coal and steel production, trade, and nuclear energy — another war in Europe would be unthinkable. Since the 1950s, this European integration project has expanded to encompass other economic sectors, a customs union, a single market in which goods, people, and capital move freely, a common agricultural policy, and a common currency (the euro). Over the last decade, EU member states have taken significant steps toward political integration as well, with decisions to develop a common foreign policy and closer police and judicial cooperation.

How Does the EU Work?

The EU represents a unique form of cooperation among sovereign states; it has been built through a series of binding treaties. EU members work together through common institutions (see next question). The EU is divided into three "pillars;" subjects and decision-making processes differ in each. Pillar One is the European Community, which encompasses economic, trade, and social policies ranging from agriculture to education.

In Pillar One areas, by far the most developed and far-reaching, members have largely pooled their national sovereignty and work together in EU institutions to set policy and promote their collective interests. Decisions in Pillar One often have a supranational character because most are made by a majority voting system. Pillar Two aims to establish a Common Foreign and Security Policy (CFSP) to permit joint action in foreign and security affairs. Pillar Three seeks to create a Justice and Home Affairs (JHA) policy to foster common internal security measures and closer police and judicial coordination. Under Pillars Two and Three, members have agreed to cooperate but decision-making is intergovernmental and by consensus. Thus, members retain more discretion and the right to veto certain measures.

How Is the EU Governed?

The EU is governed by several institutions. They do not correspond exactly to the traditional division of power in democratic governments. Rather, they embody the EU's dual supranational and intergovernmental character:

- The *European Commission* is essentially the EU's executive and has the sole right of legislative initiative. It upholds the interests of the Union as a whole and ensures that the provisions of the EU treaties are carried out properly. The 27 Commissioners are appointed by the member states for five-year terms. Each Commissioner holds a distinct portfolio (e.g., agriculture). The Commission represents the EU internationally and negotiates with third countries primarily in areas falling under Pillar One. However, the Commission is primarily an administrative entity that serves the Council of Ministers.
- The *Council of the European Union (Council of Ministers)* is comprised of ministers from the national governments. As the main decision-making body, the Council enacts legislation based on proposals put forward by the Commission. Different ministers participate depending on the subject under consideration (e.g., economics ministers could convene to discuss unemployment policy). Most decisions are made by majority vote, but some areas — such as CFSP and taxation — require unanimity. The Presidency of the Council rotates among the member states for a period of six months.
- The *European Council* brings together the Heads of State or Government of the member states and the Commission President at least twice a year. It acts principally as a strategic guide and driving force for EU policy.
- The *European Parliament* consists of 785 members. Since 1979, they have been directly elected in each member state for five-year terms under a system of proportional representation based on population. The Parliament cannot initiate legislation like national parliaments, but it shares "co-decision" power with the Council of Ministers in a number of areas, and can amend or reject the EU's budget.
- The *Court of Justice* interprets EU law and its rulings are binding; a *Court of Auditors* monitors the EU's financial management. A number of *advisory bodies* represent economic, social, and regional interests.

WHY AND HOW IS THE EU ENLARGING?

The EU sees enlargement as crucial to promoting stability and prosperity in Europe, and furthering the peaceful integration of the continent. The EU began as the European Coal and Steel Community in 1952 with six members (Belgium, France, Germany, Italy, Luxembourg, and the Netherlands). Denmark, Ireland, and the UK joined in 1973, Greece in 1981, Spain and Portugal in 1986, and Austria, Finland, and Sweden in 1995. With the end of the Cold War, the EU saw an historic opportunity to extend the political and economic benefits of membership to central and eastern Europe. On May 1, 2004, the EU welcomed 10 states (Cyprus, the Czech Republic, Estonia, Hungary, Latvia, Lithuania, Malta, Poland, Slovakia, and Slovenia) as new members. Bulgaria and Romania completed accession talks in December 2004 and acceded to the Union on January 1, 2007. Accession negotiations establish the terms under which applicants will meet and enforce EU rules and regulations. Turkey was recognized as an EU candidate in 1999 but remained in a separate category for several years as it sought to comply with the EU's political and economic criteria for membership. In October 2005, the EU opened accession talks with Turkey, but these are expected to take at least a decade to complete and have already encountered some difficulties. The EU has cautioned that the negotiations with Turkey are an "open-ended process, the outcome of which cannot be guaranteed." The EU also began accession talks with Croatia in October 2005. Macedonia was named as an EU candidate in December 2005, but no date has yet been set for the start of its membership talks.

WHAT WAS THE EU CONSTITUTION AND WHY A NEW REFORM TREATY?

In June 2004, the EU concluded work on a constitutional treaty that contained changes to the EU's governing institutions and decision-making processes. Commonly referred to as the "constitution," this new treaty grew out of previous EU efforts to institute internal reforms to enable an enlarged EU to function more effectively. The constitution also sought to boost the EU's visibility on the world stage. In order to come into effect, the constitution had to be ratified by all member states through either parliamentary approval or public referendum. The constitution's future was thrown into doubt following its rejection by French and Dutch voters in separate referendums in the spring of 2005. Reasons for its rejection varied, ranging from public unease with further EU enlargement to fears that it could lead to the creation of a European "superstate."

In December 2007, EU leaders approved a new reform treaty — the Lisbon Treaty — to essentially replace the proposed constitution. Although the term "constitution" was dropped, experts say that the Lisbon Treaty preserves over 90% of the substance of the original constitution. Major innovations include appointing a single individual to serve as president of the European Council, creating a new chief EU diplomat position, and simplifying EU voting procedures. EU officials presented the Lisbon Treaty as a document that could be ratified by parliaments, thereby avoiding risky public referendums in most EU states, except Ireland, which was required by law to hold a public vote. In June 2008, Irish voters rejected the Lisbon Treaty. Irish opponents argued that it would reduce Ireland's influence in the EU, undermine Ireland's neutrality, and eliminate its ability to set its own tax rates. EU leaders have called on the ratification process to continue in other EU states, and have given Irish officials until October 2008 to propose a way forward. EU officials hope that the Lisbon Treaty will still be able to enter into force before the next European Parliament elections in the spring of 2009.

Does the EU Have a Foreign Policy?

The EU is seeking to build a Common Foreign and Security Policy (CFSP). Past attempts to further EU political integration foundered on national sovereignty concerns and different foreign policy prerogatives. But in 1993, EU members concluded that the Union must increase its weight in world affairs to match its growing economic clout. CFSP decision-making is dominated by member states; they develop common policies in areas in which they can reach consensus, and ensure that national policies are in line with agreed EU strategies and positions (e.g., imposing sanctions on Serbia). In 1997, EU leaders proposed creating a High Representative for CFSP; in 1999, they appointed Javier Solana, NATO's former Secretary General, to the position, which is often referred to as "Mr. CFSP". Many analysts credit Solana with boosting the EU's visibility on the world stage, and with forging EU consensus on issues such as the Balkans and the Middle East peace process. Skeptics argue, however, that the EU is still far from speaking with one voice on other key foreign policy challenges. The European Commission also plays a role internationally, but should not be confused with CFSP or its High Representative. Benita Ferrero-Waldner, the External Relations

Commissioner, coordinates the Commission's diplomatic activities and manages its aid to non-member states. The Lisbon Treaty, if approved, would combine the Ferrero-Waldner and Solana posts into a single position.

DOES THE EU HAVE A DEFENSE POLICY?

The EU is also attempting to forge a European Security and Defense Policy (ESDP) to give CFSP a military backbone. Momentum for this project picked up speed in 1998, when former UK Prime Minister Tony Blair reversed Britain's traditional opposition to a European defense identity outside NATO; it intensified after NATO's 1999 Kosovo air campaign exposed serious European military deficiencies. In December 1999, the EU decided to establish an institutional decision-making framework for ESDP and a 60,000- strong rapid reaction force by 2003 — able to deploy within 60 days for at least a year — to undertake the "Petersberg tasks" (humanitarian assistance, search and rescue, peacekeeping, and peace enforcement). In June 2004, the EU agreed to enhance ESDP through the creation of several "battlegroups" of 1,500 troops each that will be able to reach trouble spots, especially in Africa, within 15 days. EU forces will not form a standing "EU army"; troops and assets at appropriate readiness levels will be drawn from existing national forces in the event of an EU operation. The EU has created three defense decision-making bodies, but improving military capabilities has been difficult, especially given flat or declining European defense budgets. Serious capability gaps exist in strategic airlift, command and control systems, intelligence, and other force multipliers.

WHAT IS THE RELATIONSHIP BETWEEN NATO AND THE EU?

The EU asserts that ESDP is intended to allow the EU to make decisions and conduct military operations "where NATO as a whole is not engaged;" ESDP is not aimed at usurping NATO's collective defense role. Most EU NATO members, led by the UK, insist that EU efforts to forge a defense arm be tied to NATO, as do U.S. policymakers. Advocates argue that building more robust European military capabilities for ESDP will also benefit the alliance. The NATO-EU relationship was formalized in December 2002, which paved the way for the implementation in March 2003 of "Berlin Plus," an arrangement permitting the

EU "assured access" to NATO operational planning capabilities and "presumed access" to NATO common assets. "Berlin Plus" was designed to help ensure close NATO-EU links, and prevent a wasteful duplication of resources. Since then, the EU has launched several crisis management missions in the Balkans, Africa, and elsewhere, with varying degrees of NATO support. Nevertheless, NATO-EU relations remain somewhat strained. This is due in part to the differences in membership in both organizations and disputes between Turkey (a NATO member) and the EU. U.S. officials have also been wary that some EU member states, traditionally led by France, would like to build a more independent EU defense arm. New French President Nicolas Sarkozy, however, has taken a more pragmatic approach; he backs a strong ESDP, but has downplayed it as an alternative to NATO and supports closer NATO-EU cooperation.

Does the EU Have a Trade Policy?

Yes. EU member states have a common external trade policy in which the European Commission negotiates trade deals with other countries and trading blocs on behalf of the Union as a whole. The EU's trade policy is one of its most well-developed and integrated policies. It evolved along with the common market, which provides for the free movement of goods within the EU, to prevent one member state from importing foreign goods at cheaper prices due to lower tariffs and then re-exporting the items to another member with higher tariffs. The scope of the common trade policy has been extended to include negotiations on services and intellectual property in some cases. The Council of Ministers has the power to establish objectives for trade negotiations and can approve or reject agreements reached by the Commission. EU rules allow the Council to make trade decisions with a weighted voting system, but in practice, the Council tends to employ consensus. The Commission and the Council work together to set the common customs tariff, guide export policy, and decide on trade protection or retaliation measures where necessary. The EU also plays a leading role in the World Trade Organization (WTO).

How Are U.S.-EU Trade Relations Doing?

The United States and the EU share the largest trade and investment relationship in the world. The value of two-way flows of goods, services, and income receipts from investment totaled $1.3 trillion in 2006. U.S. and European companies are also the biggest investors in each other's markets; total stock of two-way direct investment reached $2.2 trillion in 2006. Most of this economic relationship is harmonious, but trade tensions persist. One key dispute relates to government subsidies that the United States and EU allegedly provide to their respective civil aircraft manufacturers, Boeing and Airbus. In 2005, U.S.-EU talks to diffuse confrontation over this issue failed, and both sides have revived their complaints in the World Trade Organization (WTO). U.S.-EU conflicts over hormone-treated beef and bio-engineered food products also remain. Many analysts note that resolving U.S.-EU trade disputes has become increasingly difficult, perhaps partly because both sides are of roughly equal economic strength and neither has the ability to impose concessions on the other. Another factor may be that many disputes involve clashes in different domestic values, political priorities, and regulatory systems.

Does the United States Have a Formal Relationship with the EU?

Yes. For decades, the United States and the EU (and its progenitors) have maintained diplomatic and economic ties. Washington has strongly supported European integration, and U.S.-EU trade and investment relations are extensive. The 1990 U.S .-EU Transatlantic Declaration set out principles for greater consultation, and established regular summit and ministerial meetings. In 1995, the New Transatlantic Agenda (NTA) and the EU-U.S. Joint Action Plan provided a framework for promoting stability and democracy together, responding to global changes, and expanding world trade. The NTA also sought to strengthen individual ties across the Atlantic, and launched a number of dialogues, including ones for business leaders and legislators.

Who Are U.S. Officials' Counterparts in the EU?

At least once a year, the U.S. president meets with the president of the European Commission and the EU's rotating presidency, represented by the head of government whose country holds it at the time of the meeting. For example, at the last U.S.-EU summit in June 2008, President Bush met with Commission President José Manuel Barroso and Prime Minister Janez Jansa of Slovenia, the presidency country during the first half of 2008. The U.S. Secretary of State's most frequent interlocutors are the High Representative for CFSP, the External Relations Commissioner, and the foreign minister of the EU presidency country. The U.S. Trade Representative's key interlocutor is the European Commissioner for Trade, who directs the EU's common external trade policy. Other U.S. cabinet-level officials interact with Commission counterparts or member state ministers in Council formation as issues arise. Numerous working-level relationships between U.S. and EU officials also exist. A Delegation in Washington, DC represents the European Commission in its dealings with the U.S. government, while the U.S. Mission to the European Union represents Washington's interests in Brussels.

How Do European Countries View the EU?

All EU member states believe that the Union magnifies their political and economic clout (i.e., the sum is greater than the parts). Nevertheless, the EU has always been divided between those members that seek an "ever closer union" through greater integration and those that prefer to keep the Union on an intergovernmental footing. For example, the UK has more frequently sought to guard its national sovereignty and, along with Denmark and Sweden, does not participate in the single European currency (the euro). Another classic divide in the EU falls along big versus small state lines. Small states are often cautious of initiatives that they fear could allow EU heavyweights to dominate the Union. Another key difference relates to security postures; Austria, Finland, Ireland, and Sweden practice non-aligned foreign and defense policies, which sometimes complicates the formulation of common European positions in these areas. In addition, the recent rounds of EU enlargement to the east have brought in many new members with histories of Soviet domination, which often color their views on issues ranging from EU reform to relations with Russia; at times, such differences have caused frictions with older EU member states and have slowed EU decision making.

In: The Financial Crisis and the European Union ISBN: 978-1-60741-987-7
Editor: Klaus G. Efenhoff

Chapter 3

THE FINANCIAL CRISIS: IMPACT ON AND RESPONSE BY THE EUROPEAN UNION*

James K. Jackson†

ABSTRACT

According to the most recent National Threat Assessment, the global financial crisis and its geopolitical implications pose the primary near-term security concern of the United States. Over the short run, both the EU and the United States are attempting to resolve the financial crisis while stimulating domestic demand to stem the economic downturn. These efforts have born little progress so far as the economic recession and the financial crisis have become reinforcing events, causing EU governments to forge policy responses to both crises. In addition, both the United States and the EU likely will confront the prospect of growing economic and political instability in Eastern Europe and elsewhere over the impact of the economic recession on restive populations. In the long run, the United States and the EU likely will search for a regulatory scheme that provides for greater stability while not inadvertently offering advantages to any one country or group. Throughout

* This is an edited, reformatted and augmented version of a Congressional Research Service publication, dated March 9, 2009.

† jjackson@crs.loc.gov, 7-7751

the crisis, the European Central Bank and other central banks have assumed a critical role as the primary institutions with the necessary political and economic clout to respond effectively. Within Europe, national governments, private firms, and international organizations have varied in their response to the financial crisis, reflecting differing views over the proper policy course to pursue and the unequal effects of the financial crisis and the economic downturn. Initially, some EU members preferred to address the crisis on a case-by-case basis. As the crisis has persisted, however, leaders have begun looking for a systemic approach that ultimately may affect the drive within Europe toward greater economic integration.

Within the United States, Congress has appropriated funds to help recapitalize financial institutions, and adopted several economic stimulus measures. In addition, Congress likely will be involved in efforts to reshape institutions and frameworks for international cooperation and coordination in financial markets. European governments are also adopting fiscal measures to stimulate their economies and wrestling with failing banks. The financial crisis has demonstrated that financial markets are highly interdependent and that extensive networks link financial markets across national borders, which is pressing EU governments to work together to find a mutually reinforcing solution. Unlike the United States, however, where the federal government can legislate policies that are consistent across all 50 States, the EU process gives each EU member a great deal of discretion to decide how they will regulate and supervise financial markets within their borders. The limits of this system may well be tested as the EU and others search for a regulatory framework that spans a broad number of national markets. Governments that have expended considerable resources utilizing fiscal and monetary policy tools to stabilize the financial system and to provided a boost to their economies may be required to be increasingly more inventive in providing yet more stimulus to their economies and face political unrest in domestic populations. Attention likely will also focus on those governments that are viewed as not expending economic resources commensurate with the size of their economies to stimulate economic growth.

OVERVIEW

Some members of the European Union[1] (EU) initially viewed the financial crisis as a purely American phenomenon. That view has changed as economic activity in the EU has declined at a fast pace over a short period of time. Making matters worse, global trade has declined sharply, eroding prospects for European exports providing a safety valve for domestic industries that are cutting output. In addition, public protests, sparked by rising rates of unemployment and concerns over the growing financial and economic turmoil, are increasing the political stakes for EU governments and their leaders. The global economic crisis is straining the ties that bind together the members of the EU and could present a significant challenge to the ideals of solidarity and common interests. In addition, the longer the economic downturn persists, the greater the prospects are that international pressure will mount against those governments that are perceived as not carrying their share of the responsibility for stimulating their economies to an extent that is commensurate with the size of their economy. According to Dennis Blair, Director of U.S. National Intelligence, the global financial crisis and its geopolitical implications pose, "the primary near-term security concern of the United States." In addition, he said, "The longer it takes for the [economic] recovery to begin, the greater the likelihood of serious damage to U.S. strategic interests. Roughly a quarter of the countries in the world have already experienced low- level instability such as government changes because of the current slowdown."[2]

Various EU governments have had to expend public resources to rescue failing banks, in addition to protecting depositors and utilizing monetary and fiscal tools to support banks, to unfreeze credit markets, and to stimulate economic growth. These efforts have born modest progress so far as the economic recession and the financial crisis have become reinforcing events, which are forcing EU governments to forge policy responses to both crises. As the loss of real and financial wealth worsens, EU governments have worked both independently and in concert to address the immediate requirements of protecting financial institutions and improving access to credit by households and businesses. The differential effects of the economic downturn, however, are dividing the wealthier countries of the Eurozone[3] from the poorer countries within the EU and in East Europe and are compounding efforts to respond to the financial crisis and the economic recession. Once the immediate issues are resolved, EU governments likely will address long-term solutions to regulating and supervising financial markets. EU governments have found some common ground for solutions to the financial crisis, but the financial crisis has demonstrated that the international scope of financial activities often cause firms operating in their respective jurisdictions to compete over the highly lucrative financial services sector. In the long run, they likely will search for a regulatory scheme that provides for greater stability while not inadvertently offering advantages to any one group.

For the United States and the members of the European Union the stakes are high. Over the short run, both the EU and the United States are attempting to stop the downward spiral in the financial system, improve the financial architecture, and restore balanced economic growth. Over the long run, they likely will search for a regulatory scheme that provides for greater stability while not inadvertently offering advantages to any one country. The financial crisis and the economic downturn have become global events and likely will dominate the attention of policymakers for some time to come. Governments that have expended considerable resources utilizing fiscal and monetary policy tools to stabilize the financial system and to provide a boost to their economies may be required to be increasingly more inventive in providing yet more stimulus to their economies and face political unrest in domestic populations.

EU members are also concerned over the impact the financial crisis and the economic recession are having on the economies of East Europe and prospects for political instability[4] as well as future prospects for market reforms. Worsening economic conditions in East European countries could compound the current problems facing financial institutions in EU members. While mutual necessity may eventually dictate a more unified position among EU members and increased efforts to aid East European economies, some observers are concerned these actions may come too late to forestall another blow to the EU economies and to the United States. Governments elsewhere in Europe, such as Iceland and Latvia, have collapsed as a result of public protests over the way their governments have handled their economies during the crisis, and the International Monetary Fund has issued emergency loans to Hungary and Ukraine. The World Bank in a joint effort with the European Bank for Reconstruction and Development and the European Investment Bank announced on February 27, 2009 that they were providing $31 billion over two years to assist ailing banks and businesses in Eastern and Central Europe [5].

East European countries are experiencing a sharp depreciation in their currencies relative to the Euro and the economic crisis likely will cause their government deficits to rise, undermining the efforts of some of the countries to join the Eurozone [6]. Banks in the EU have nearly $1.5 trillion in assets potentially at risk in Central and Eastern Europe. The data in table 1 include the exposure of the major Western European banks for East European countries and the Russian Federation. Despite this exposure to banks in Eastern Europe, EU leaders, at a meeting on March 1, 2009 reportedly could not agree on a common approach to the financial crisis and rejected a call by Hungary for financial support for Eastern Europe. Even the East European participants could not bridge their differences and present a unified approach to the EU. Some East European countries pushed for substantial financial assistance from the EU, while other countries expressed little interest in receiving financial assistance [7].

Table 1. Major Western European Banks' Claims on Central and Eastern Europe (in billions of U.S. dollars)

	Austria	Belgium	France	Germany	Italy	Netherlands	Sweden	Total
Belarus	$2.1	$0.1	$0.2	$0.9	$0.2	$0.1	$0.0	$3.6
Bulgaria	5.7	2.0	3.6	2.8	8.1	0.7	0.0	22.9
Czech. Rep.	65.1	56.7	38.6	12.7	19.0	6.2	0.2	198.5
Estonia	0.3	0.1	0.1	1.1	0.4	0.0	32.7	34.7
Hungary	38.3	18.7	11.9	37.9	29.3	5.6	0.3	142.0
Latvia	0.8	0.0	0.4	4.8	1.4	0.0	25.0	32.4
Lithuania	0.3	0.1	0.4	3.8	0.7	0.0	28.9	34.2
Poland	17.2	25.2	22.9	55.4	54.4	41.2	8.1	224.4
Romania	46.5	1.2	17.6	3.8	12.9	11.0	0.2	93.2
Russian Fed.	23.9	10.3	34.7	49.5	25.7	25.5	9.9	179.5
Slovakia	33.2	10.9	6.4	4.1	23.6	6.7	0.2	85.1
Ukraine	12.9	0.8	10.6	5.0	4.9	3.7	5.4	43.3
Total	246.3	126.1	147.4	181.8	180.6	100.7	110.9	3.8

The crisis has underscored the growing interdependence between financial markets and between the U.S. and European economies. As such, the synchronized nature of the current economic downturn probably means that neither the United States nor the EU is likely to emerge from the financial crisis or the economic downturn alone. The United States and the EU share a mutual interest in developing a sound financial architecture to improve supervision and regulation of individual institutions and of international markets. This issue includes developing the organization and structures within national economies that can provide oversight of the different segments of the highly complex financial system. This oversight is viewed by many as critical to the future of the financial system because financial markets generally are considered to play an indispensible role in allocating capital and facilitating economic activity.

In the months ahead, Congress and the Obama Administration likely will consider a number of proposals to restructure the supervisory and regulatory responsibilities over the broad-based financial sector within the United States. At the same time, such international organizations, as the G-20, the Financial Stability Forum, the International Monetary Fund, the Organization for Economic Cooperation and Development, and the Bank for International Settlements likely will offer their own prescriptions for the international financial markets.

Financial Architecture

As policymakers address this issue, they likely will weigh the costs and benefits of centralizing supervisory responsibilities into a few key entities, such as the Federal Reserve, or dispersing them more widely across a number of different entities. A centralized approach may avoid the haphazard way in which certain complex financial markets and transactions went largely unregulated. On the other hand, a broader dispersion of supervisory responsibilities may yield a more specialized approach to market supervision. In the United States, the Federal Reserve holds a monopoly over the conduct of monetary policy, mainly as a means of keeping such policy- making independent of political interests. The Federal Reserve also shares regulatory and supervisory responsibilities with a number of different agencies that are more directly accountable to elected officials and are subject to change. The EU system, however, is different from the U.S. system in ways that may complicate efforts at coordination. For instance, the European Central Bank is not strictly comparable to the Federal Reserve in both scope of its regulatory role and its role in supervising banks. In the EU system each EU member has its own institutional and legal framework for regulating its banking market, and national supervisory authorities are organized differently by each EU country with different powers and accountability.

On various occasions over the past several months, EU leaders have discussed the need to develop a common set of rules that could help regulate financial markets and prevent another financial crisis. What has emerged, however, is a lack of consensus over the details of such a regulatory scheme. On February 22, 2009, leaders and Finance Ministers from Germany, the United Kingdom, France, Italy, Spain, the Netherlands, Czech Republic, and Luxembourg met in Berlin to map out a common approach to overhauling financial rules in preparation for the G20 meeting in London on April 2, 2009. A position paper prepared by German Finance Minister Peer Steinbruck set out five areas of discussion for the European leaders: 1) transparency and accountability; 2) enhancing "sound regulation; 3) promoting integrity in financial markets; 4) strengthening international cooperation; and 5) reforming international financial institutions. Beyond these vague goals, the group has not been able to provide a detailed roadmap of how to achieve a new financial architecture, or to gain a unified approach within the broader membership of the EU.

The European leaders also considered proposals for the G20 meeting that would require banks to increase their capital resources in periods of faster economic growth. Reportedly, the Ministers also discussed the growing economic problems in Eastern European countries, tax havens, trade protectionism, and a $500 billion fund for the International Monetary Fund to deal with economic crises. Following the formal talks, German Chancellor Merkel spoke in favor of adopting global regulations for financial markets and hedge funds. In a statement released on behalf of all of the leaders, Chancellor Merkel said, "All financial markets, products, and participants, including hedge funds and other private pools of capital which may pose a systemic risk must be subjected to appropriate oversight or regulation" [8].

The current financial and economic crises have exposed deep philosophical differences among EU members over the most effective policy course to pursue to address these two crises. EU members have addressed the financial crisis independently and in concert through the EU organization, reflecting the dual nature of the EU system. Unlike the United States, where the Federal government can implement policies that are applied systematically across all 50 States, EU-wide actions reflect compromise among national authorities. As a result, the national authorities exercise considerable freedom in implementing EU Directives and in charting their own response to the crisis. For instance, EU members agreed to support an EU-wide fiscal stimulus to counter the economic downturn. The worsening economic conditions in Europe, however, have not been felt evenly across all EU members, and their response has exposed differences in economic philosophies that have blunted a coordinated approach. EU members also have responded differently to helping banks reduce their exposure to so-called toxic loans, because in the current environment their market value cannot be determined. The efforts by some EU members to address this issue has pushed the EU to consider an EU-wide approach.

Within the EU, however, integration of the financial services sector across borders has been uneven, with integration progressing faster in the money, bond, and equity markets, and slowest in the banking sector where many of the policy changes likely will be focused. According to the European Central Bank,[9] retail banking services remain segmented along national lines as a result of differences in national tax laws, costs of national registration and compliance, and cultural preferences. Nevertheless, cross-border mergers and acquisitions within Europe have played an important role in internationalizing banking groups, which has led to significant cross-border banking activity. Integration within the banking sector in Europe also has increased since the European Community adopted the euro as the EU's single currency.

The EU response to the two crises has been complicated further by a number of factors, including the need to mesh new proposals with such existing EU Directives as the Stability and Growth Pact[10], the Lisbon Principles[11], and the Financial Services Action Plan [12]. The EU structure gives the individual members considerable latitude to formulate their own policies in response to crises. In some cases, this has meant that the EU has had to adopt policies that have been implemented by some of its members to prevent a sort of EU-wide competition. For instance, EU members were pressed to support a broad set of measures to increase the guarantees on bank accounts for depositors in response to actions by Ireland, Greece, and Germany. Some EU members are also considering procedures to deal with the bad loans of banks within their jurisdictions, which has pushed the EU as a whole to follow suit and consider the best approach to deal with the toxic loans of EU banks. This and other issues have exposed sharp differences among the EU members over the best approach to deal with financial market reforms and economic stimulus measures. These differences may well become more pronounced as multilateral discussions shift from addressing the general goal of containing the financial crisis to the more contentious issues of specific market reforms, regulations, and supervision.

Economic Performance

Estimates developed by the International Monetary Fund in January 2009 provide a rough indicator of the impact the financial crisis and an economic recession are having on the performance of major advanced countries. Economic growth in Europe is expected to slow by nearly 2% in 2009 to post a 0.2% drop in the rate of economic growth, while the threat of inflation is expected to lessen, as indicated in table 2. Economic growth, as represented by gross domestic product (GDP), is expected to register a negative 1.6% rate for the United States in 2009, while the euro area countries could experience a combined negative rate of 2.0%, down from a projected rate of growth of 1.2% in 2008. The sharp drop in the prices of oil and other commodities in the later part of 2008 may have helped improve the rate of economic growth, but the length and depth of the economic downturn likely well mean that the IMF projections prove to be too optimistic when the final data for 2009 are known. Indeed, in mid-February, the European Union announced that the rate of economic growth in the EU in the fourth quarter of 2008 had slowed to an annual rate of negative 6% [13].

Table 2. Projections of Economic Growth in Various Countries and Areas (real GDP growth, in percent change)

	2007	2008	2009	2010
	Actual		Projected	
World	5.2	3.4	0.5	3.0
United States	2.0	1.1	-1.6	1.6
Advanced Economies	2.7	1.0	-2.0	1.1
Emerging Economies	8.3	6.3	3.3	5.0
European Union	3.1	1.3	-1.8	0.5
Euro Area	2.6	1.0	-2.0	0.2
France	2.2	0.8	-1.9	0.7
Germany	2.5	1.3	-2.5	0.1
Italy	1.5	-0.6	-2.1	-0.1
Spain	2.4	-0.3	-2.6	0.6
United Kingdom	3.0	0.7	-2.8	0.2
Non-EU advanced	4.6	1.9	-2.4	2.2
Japan	2.4	-0.3	-2.6	0.6
Canada	2.7	0.6	-1.2	1.6

The Financial Crisis and the European Union

The cause and effects of the current financial crisis likely will be debated for years to come. This report does not attempt to provide a complete explanation of the causes of the financial crisis, since other CRS Reports address these issues [14]. While different individuals and organizations view the crisis from different perspectives, one way to view the crisis is as a series of policy events proceeding through four periods where the policy responses differed [15]. The periods are not necessarily discretely identifiable, because they overlap with other periods, or the policy responses have been repeated as the financial crisis has persisted. This has been especially true as the financial crisis has deepened over time and as the economic downturn and the financial crisis have become reinforcing events, compounding efforts to resolve either crisis.

The first phase of the crisis represents the early build-up to the crisis in which policymakers responded in an *ad hoc* manner to assist individually troubled banks and financial institutions. In the second phase, national governments, primarily through central banks, moved to address issues of liquidity that arose from wide-spread concerns over the viability of the financial system, rather than the more narrow concerns of individual institutions. In the third phase, government finance ministries adopted policies to address issues of solvency as banks and other financial firms attempted to deleverage their positions by reducing their holdings of troubled assets and as credit markets essentially shut down. In the fourth phase, governments, through finance ministries and legislative bodies, shifted to address growing concerns over the economic downturn that has worsened the financial crisis.

According to reports by the International Monetary Fund (IMF) and the European Central Bank (ECB), many of the factors that led to the financial crisis in the United States created a similar crisis in Europe [16]. Essentially low interest rates and an expansion of financial and investment opportunities that arose from aggressive credit expansion, growing complexity in mortgage securitization, and loosening in underwriting standards combined with expanded linkages among national financial centers to spur a broad expansion in credit and economic growth. This rapid rate of growth pushed up the values of equities, commodities, and real estate. Over time, the combination of higher commodity prices and rising housing costs pinched consumers' budgets, and they began reducing their expenditures. One consequence of this drop in consumer spending was a slowdown in economic activity and, eventually, a contraction in the prices of housing. In turn, the decline in the prices of housing led to a large-scale downgrade in the ratings of subprime mortgage-backed securities and the closing of a number of hedge funds with subprime exposure. Concerns over the pricing of risk in the market for subprime mortgage-backed securities spread to other financial markets, including to structured securities more generally and the interbank money market. Problems spread quickly throughout the financial sector to include financial guarantors as the markets turned increasingly dysfunctional over fears of under valued assets.

PHASE I: BUILD-UP

The first phase of the financial crisis is identified with a loss of confidence in credit markets that was associated with a downturn in the U.S. housing market caused primarily by rising defaults in subprime mortgages. In this stage, EU governments generally responded on a case-by-case basis, without a role for the broader Community. A sharp downturn in mortgage markets generally would be expected to have a negative impact on parts of the economy, but the current financial crisis quickly evolved into a more general liquidity crisis that spread well beyond the sub-prime mortgage market. Initially, only highly leveraged banks, investment firms, and other financial services providers seemed to be affected by the credit problems. During this phase in the United States, the Federal Deposit Insurance Corporation took control of IndyMac Bank.

The financial crisis that began in the United States as a result of a downturn in residential property values quickly spread to European banks through effects felt in the market for asset- backed commercial paper (ABCP) [17]. European banks were either directly holding the securities or they were holding them indirectly through conduits and structured investment vehicles with similar holdings. As the ABCP market collapsed, banks holding such securities were forced to step in with additional funding, which squeezed liquidity in the global financial market through the interbank market. Over time, banks and other financial firms found that it was impossible to price the value of assets that were being used to back commercial paper. During this phase, the British government nationalized housing lender Northern Rock and Bradford & Bingley, a mortgage lender. Belgium, France, and Luxembourg governments and shareholders provided capital to Dexia, the world's largest lender to municipalities, and Belgian, Dutch, and Luxembourg governments injected $16.4 billion into banking and insurance company Fortis to head off the first major bank crisis in the Euro area.

PHASE II: LIQUIDITY ISSUES

In the second phase, policy shifted from an *ad hoc* focus on the fate of individual firms to concerns over troubled markets as central banks intervened to lower interest rates, to provide liquidity, and to provide foreign currency. In the United States, as generally is the case in most countries, the Federal Reserve, or the central bank, holds a monopoly over the conduct of monetary policy, mainly as a means of keeping such policy-making independent from political pressure. Normally, it is not the role of the central bank to be the main provider of liquidity, but that role falls to the central banks as lenders of last resort during periods of financial crisis. In addition, central banks generally share regulatory and supervisory responsibilities, including providing assistance to individual firms or helping banks deleverage, with a number of different agencies that are more directly accountable to elected officials and are subject to change.

During this phase, governments attempted to stabilize the financial markets by expanding insurance on guarantees for depositors and, in some cases, guarantees for banks. Central banks also engaged in direct injections of capital to support the balance sheets of banks and removed some distressed assets from banks by acquiring the assets. Efforts to acquire distressed assets from the banks, however, raised questions concerning the value of the assets, since, in most cases, the value of the assets had fallen below the value indicated on the balance sheets of the banks. The Bank for International Settlements (BIS) indicates that governments in Europe varied their responses to the financial crisis, as indicated in table 3. In addition, the BIS indicates that there are considerable differences in the design and implementation of the rescue efforts and in the way foreign depositors are treated in the case of a bank failure.

In this phase, Iceland was especially hard hit by the financial crisis, with major Icelandic banks completely shutting down for a period of time [18]. On November 19, 2008, Iceland and the International Monetary Fund (IMF) finalized an agreement on an economic stabilization program supported by a $2.1 billion two-year standby arrangement from the IMF [19]. Following the IMF decision, Denmark, Finland, Norway, and Sweden agreed to provide an additional $2.5 billion. On January 26, 2009, public protests against the Icelandic government's handling of the crisis and the economy caused Iceland's Prime Minister Haarde to resign and the coalition government to fall.

Table 3. Elements of Banking System Rescue Plans in European Countries

		Guarantee of wholesale liability			
Country	Expansion of retail deposit insurance	New debt	Existing debt	Capital injections	Asset purchases
Austria	X	X		X	
Belgium	X	X		X	
Denmark	X	X	X		
Finland	X				
France		X		X	
Germany	X	X		X	X
Greece	X	X		X	X
Ireland	X	X	X		
Italy		X		X	
Netherlands	X	X		X	
Norway					X
Portugal	X	X			
Spain	X	X		X	X
Sweden	X	X		X	X
Switzerland				X	X
United Kingdom	X	X		X	X

Source: Fender, Ingo, and Jacob Gyntelberg, Overview: global financial Crisis Spurs Unprecedented Policy Actions, Quarterly Review, Bank for International Settlements, December 2008, p. 11.

Central Bank Operations

During this phase, U.S. mortgage markets continued to deteriorate, prompting the U.S. Treasury and Federal Reserve to engineer the acquisition of Bear Stearns by JPMorgan Chase and to announce that it was taking over the Federal National Mortgage Association (Fannie Mae) and the Federal Home Loan Mortgage Corporation (Freddie Mac). Soon after this takeover, Lehman Brothers filed for bankruptcy, which led to a more wide-spread crisis of confidence, and which, in turn, led credit markets to freeze up and led to a lack of liquidity. Given Lehman's far-reaching exposure in the financial markets, its collapse likely would have had a negative impact on the financial markets under normal circumstances, but the impact was magnified by underlying weaknesses in the markets that had been building over time. In particular, Lehman was heavily involved in the $57 trillion credit default swap (CDS)[20] market. Lehman's bankruptcy triggered clauses in

CDS contracts that referenced Lehman, and it terminated contracts that Lehman had entered into as a counterparty [21]. Lehman also originated commercial paper and other forms of short term debt that a number of European banks held through Lehman's global presence. As investors scrambled to redeem commercial paper, the Federal Reserve stepped in to the money markets and purchased commercial paper and other short term money market securities. Particularly hard hit by the Lehman bankruptcy was AIG (American International Group), which had been closely tied to the CDSs offered by Lehman. The Federal Reserve arranged for a $85 billion credit facility in exchange for an 80% equity stake in AIG.

Various governments, through their central banks, injected capital directly into banks and other financial firms during this phase to keep firms from failing and to arrange mergers by providing liquidity. The British government arranged for Halifax Bank of Scotland (HBOS) to be acquired by the Lloyds Banking Group. In the United States, the Office of Thrift of Supervision seized Washington Mutual Bank from Washington Mutual, Inc. and arranged for its sale to JPMorgan Chase. The Federal Reserve also approved the transformation of Goldman Sachs and Morgan Stanley into bank holding companies.

According to a paper prepared by staff at the International Monetary Fund (IMF) [22], one of the key issues facing central banks during the crisis has been distinguishing between troubled markets and troubled institutions. Troubled institutions can be dealt with on a case-by-case basis, as was done in the initial stages of the financial crisis. Troubled markets, however, require a more coordinated approach since the effects can span a range of countries and financial markets. The authors also concluded that central banks were able to respond quickly to the financial crisis as a result of various aspects of their operational framework that allowed them to respond without fundamentally changing their basic monetary policy. While it is important for central banks to be flexible when responding to a crisis, the study emphasized, central banks, "cannot come to be seen as the market maker of last resort in all markets nor the lender of last resort for all institutions." The authors concluded that central bank policies should strike a balance between supporting the financial system during times of crisis and setting in motion the seeds of future crises. Also, the study indicated that certain types of central bank mechanisms proved to be more effective in providing liquidity and in coping with significant turbulence in the financial markets.

The European Central Bank provided large quantities of reserves through routine short-term open-market operations and through longer-term open market operations. Unlike the Federal Reserve, which normally conducts open market operations with a small set of primary dealers against a narrow range of highly liquid collateral, the ECB routinely conducts open market operations with a wide range of counterparties against a broad range of collateral. The ECB extended this strategy during this phase of the financial crisis with a longer term refinancing operation [23]. This greater flexibility, compared with the Federal Reserve, reportedly made it possible for the ECB to provide liquidity within its existing framework without resorting to extraordinary measures [24]. During this phase, the UK's Financial Services Authority arranged for the sale of a large part of Bradford & Bingley to the Spanish bank Grupo Santander, while Fortis, a banking and insurance company received a capital injection from the Belgian, Dutch, and Luxembourg governments.

During this phase, the British Government announced a $850 billion multi-part plan to rescue its banking sector from the financial crisis, known as the Stability and Reconstruction Plan. The key feature of the plan, as promoted by British Prime Minister Gordon Brown, has the central government acquiring preferred shares in distressed banks for a specified amount of time, rather than acquiring the non-performing loans of the banks. The announcement of the Plan followed a day when British banks lost more than $25 billion on the London Stock Exchange. The biggest loser was the Royal Bank of Scotland, whose shares fell 39%, representing $15 billion, of lost value. In the downturn, other British banks lost substantial amounts of their value, including the Halifax Bank of Scotland which was in the process of being acquired by Lloyds TSB. The British plan is comprised of four parts:

- First was a coordinated cut in key interest rates of 50 basis points, or one-half of one percent (0.5) with the Bank of England, the Federal Reserve, and the European Central Bank all participating.
- Second was an announcement of an investment facility of $87 billion implemented in two stages to acquire the Tier 1 capital, or preferred stock, in "eligible" banks and building societies (financial institutions that specialize on mortgage financing) in order to recapitalize the firms. Under the financial plan, eight British banks – Abbey, RBS, Barclays, Hallifax Bank of Scotland, HSBC (Hong Kong and Shanghai Banking Corporation), Lloyds TSB, Standard Chartered, and Nationwide Building Society – signed up to participate in the recapitalization effort.
- Third, the British Government agreed to make available to those institutions participating in the recapitalization scheme up to $436 billion in guarantees on new short- and medium-term debt to assist in refinancing maturing funding obligations as they fall due for terms up to three years.

- Fourth, the British Government announced that it would make available $352 billion through the Special Liquidity Scheme [25] to improve liquidity in the banking industry [26].

In addition to this four-part plan, the Bank of England announced that it had developed three new proposals for its money market operations. First, was the establishment of Operational Standing Facilities that are aimed at addressing technical problems and imbalances in the operation of money markets and payments facilities, although they did not provide financial support. Second, the establishment of a Discount Window Facility which allows banks to borrow government bonds or, at the Bank's discretion, cash, against a wide range of eligible collateral to provide liquidity insurance to commercial banks in stress. Third, a permanent open market for long-tem repurchase agreements (securities sold for cash with an agreement to repurchase the securities at a specified time) against broader classes of collateral to offer banks additional tools for managing their liquidity [27]. The plan was quickly implemented with the UK government taking a controlling interest in the Royal Bank of Scotland (RBS) and Hallifax Bank of Scotland (HBOS).

At the euro area summit on October 12, 2008, the euro area countries, along with the United Kingdom, urged all European governments to adopt a common set of principles to address the financial crisis [28]. The measures the nations supported were largely in line with those that had been proposed by the United Kingdom and included:

- Recapitalization: governments promised to provide funds to banks that might be struggling to raise capital and pledged to pursue wide-ranging restructuring of the leadership of those banks that are turning to the government for capital.
- State ownership: governments indicated that they will buy shares in the banks that are seeking recapitalization.
- Government debt guarantees: guarantees offered for any new debts, including inter-bank loans, issued by the banks in the euro zone area.
- Improved regulations: the governments agreed to encourage regulations to permit assets to be valued on their risk of default, instead of their current market price.

In addition to these measures, EU leaders agreed on October 16, 2008, to set up a crisis unit and they agreed to a monthly meeting to improve financial oversight [29]. Jose Manuel Barroso, President of the European Commission, urged EU members to develop a "fully integrated solution" to address the global financial crisis, consistent with France's support for a strong international organization to oversee the financial markets. The EU members expressed their support for the current approach within the EU, which makes each EU member responsible for developing and implementing its own national regulations regarding supervision over financial institutions. The European Council stressed the need to strengthen the supervision of the European financial sector. As a result, the EU statement urged the EU members to develop a "coordinated supervision system at the European level."[30] This approach likely will be tested as a result of failed talks with the credit derivatives industry in Europe. In early January 2009, an EUsponsored working group reported that it had failed to get a commitment from the credit derivatives industry to use a central clearing house for credit default swaps. As an alternative, the European Commission reportedly is considering adopting a set of rules for EU members that would require banks and other users of the CDS markets to use a central clearing house within the EU as a way of reducing risk [31].

Interest Rates

On October 8, 2008, central banks in the United States, the Eurozone, the United Kingdom, Canada, Sweden, and Switzerland staged a coordinated cut in interest rates to improve liquidity, and they announced that they had a plan of action to address the ever-widening financial crisis [32][2].

Soon after, the U.S. Treasury, in coordination with the Federal Reserve, announced its Capital Purchase Program as part of its Troubled Asset Relief Program and arranged for an injection of capital in exchange for equity shares into eight major U.S. banks [33]. On October 29, 2008, the U.S. Federal Reserve cut key interest rates by half a percentage point, a move that was matched by China and Norway [34]. In response to these cuts, on November 6, 2008, the Bank of England cut its key interest rates by 1.5 percent points to 3%. The cut was three times larger than any seen since the central bank's monetary policy committee was established in 1997 [35]. At the same time, the European Central Bank (ECB), which sets interest rates for the 16 members of the Eurozone, cut its interest rates by half a percentage point to 3.25% [36]. The Czech Central Bank also cut its rates by a larger than expected three-quarters of a percentage point, while the Swiss National Bank lowered its rates by one-half of a percentage point. The cut in rates came as the IMF published an emergency update of its economic forecasts, predicting that the economies of the developed countries would shrink by 0.3% in 2009, down from a projection released in October that growth among the most developed economies would increase by 0.5%.

Currency Swap Facilities

In addition to reducing interest rates and providing liquidity by injecting capital directly into banks, the Federal Reserve and other central banks in Europe and elsewhere expanded short-term bilateral currency swap facilities by $180 billion to compensate for a dollar liquidity crisis. The dollar is used widely in international trade transactions and as a reserve currency by other central banks. The dollar is also used by many financial institutions outside the United States that have substantially increased their dollar investments, including loans to nonbanks and purchases of asset-backed securities issued by U.S. firms. Most financial institutions outside the United States have relied on interbank and other wholesale markets to obtain dollars. As credit markets seized up, however, these institutions found they did not have access to short-term dollar financing. European banks, in particular, had difficulties obtaining US dollar funding. Preceding the financial crisis, European banks had vastly expanded their accumulation of dollars in the interbank market and from official monetary authorities that had acquired dollar-denominated assets. In essence, European banks borrowed dollars short term in the interbank market in order to finance a rapid growth in investments in dollar-denominated assets with varying maturities in assets held by non-banks, such as asset-backed commercial paper, which left European banks with large short-term US dollar funding requirements. Such constant refinancing contributed to the squeeze in liquidity and to problems in obtaining dollars in the foreign exchange market and in cross-country currency swap markets [37].

The principal tool the Federal Reserve and the European Central Bank used to counter the currency shortage is a temporary currency swap, which allows central banks to borrow currency from each other in order to relend the currencies to banks in their jurisdictions. Typically, inter-central bank foreign exchange swap arrangements are used to support foreign exchange market intervention, rather than to alleviate shortages of foreign exchange in the short-term funding market. Prior to September 2008, the Federal Reserve had established inter-central bank currency swap lines with the Swiss National Bank and with the European Central Bank to deliver U.S. dollar funds, complimenting the Federal Reserve's Term Auction Facility. Between September 2008 and November 2008, the Federal

Reserve established such arrangements with more than a dozen other central banks [38].

In addition to shortages of dollars, there have also been shortages of euros and Swiss francs. During the period when the European Central Bank was concluding swap arrangements with the Federal Reserve, it was also establishing currency swaps with the Czech central bank, the National Bank of Denmark, and the National Bank of Poland. Central banks in Europe responded to the currency shortage by providing currency from their own foreign exchange reserves and by borrowing from other central banks, principally from the central bank that issued the currency.

Depositor Guarantees

Ireland, Greece, and Germany also increased their guarantees to deposit holders to improve liquidity in the financial system, a move that was adopted by the EU as a whole to curtail a form of regulatory competition for depositors. The International Monetary Fund also approved a short- term liquidity facility to assist banks facing liquidity problems. The G-7 [39] group of countries met to discuss a coordinated approach to the crisis [40], followed by the Euro area summit, at which the Euro area countries urged all European governments to help recapitalize banks, to have governments buy shares in banks, if needed, to guarantee the debt of banks, and to improve bank regulations [41].

On December 4, 2008, European central banks initiated another round of cuts in interest rates. The ECB cut its key rate by three-quarters of a percentage point to 2.5%, representing the largest one-day rate move in the bank's 10-year history. In turn, the Bank of England cut its key rate by a full percentage point to 2%. Sweden's central bank also cut interest rates by 1.75 percentage points to 2%, the largest single cut in rates in 16 years [42]. On January 8, 2009, the Bank of England reduced its Official Bank Rate by 0.5 percentage points to 1.5% [43]. In addition, on February 5, 2009, the Bank of England announced an additional cut in its official bank rate by 0.5% to 1.0% to stimulate economic growth [44]. On January 15, 2009, the ECB President Jean-Claude Trichet announced that the bank had cut its rates by 0.5% to 2.0% as a result of lower inflationary pressures and weakening economic prospects due to reduced exports and lower domestic demand within the EU countries [45]. In summing up, Trichet indicated that the reasoning behind the ECB's decision was based on a number of factors:

> This takes into account the latest economic data releases and survey information, which add clear further evidence to the assessment that the euro area is experiencing a significant slowdown, largely related to the effects of the intensification and broadening of the financial turmoil. Both global demand and euro area demand are likely to be dampened for a protracted period. All in all, the level of uncertainty remains exceptionally high [46].

PHASE III: SOLVENCY AND DELEVERAGING

In the third phase, the lack of confidence in credit markets and a lack of liquidity also sparked concerns over the adequacy of capital provisions of financial institutions and concerns over the solvency of banks and other financial firms. During this phase, financial firms attempted to deleverage by reducing the amount of troubled assets they held on their balance sheets. At the same time, the stocks of most financial firms in the United States and in Europe dropped markedly, and the value of their assets deteriorated, which weakened the financial position of an even larger number of firms. In this phase, intervention by central banks continued, but national governments also began to intervene, typically through their respective Treasury departments, to take control of insolvent banks or otherwise to provide financial assistance. The U.S. Congress passed the Troubled Assets Relief Program as part of the Emergency Economic Stabilization Act (P.L. 110-343) initially intended to acquire up to $700 billion in troubled mortgage-related securities [47]. As the financial crisis persisted, U.S. Treasury Secretary Geithner announced on February 9, 2009, that the Financial Stability Plan that was being prepared at that time by the Treasury Department provided a "full arsenal of financial tools and the resources commensurate" to stress test banks; to provide for a public-private investment fund; to provide funds for consumer and business lending; and to ensure greater transparency, accountability, and monitoring of banks [48].

The "European Framework for Action"

On October 29, 2008, the European Commission released its "European Framework for Action" as a way to coordinate the actions of the 27 members of the European Union in addressing the financial crisis [49]. On November 16, 2008, the Commission announced a more detailed plan that brings together short-term goals to address the current economic downturn with the longer-term goals on growth and jobs that are integral to the Lisbon Strategy for Growth and Jobs that was adopted by the EU in 2000 and recast in 2005. The short-term plan focuses on a three-part approach to an overall EU recovery action plan/framework. The three parts to the EU framework are: 1) a new financial market architecture at the EU-level; 2) dealing with the impact on the real economy; and 3) a global response to the financial crisis.

- **A new financial market architecture at the EU level**. The basis of this architecture involves implementing measures that EU members have announced as well as providing for: 1) continued support for the financial system from the European Central Bank and other central banks; 2) rapid and consistent implementation on the bank rescue plan that has been established by the member states; and 3) decisive measures that are designed to contain the crisis from spreading to all of the member states. As the financial system is stabilized, the next step is to restructure the banking sector and to return banks to the private sector. Proposals include: deposit guarantees and capital requirements; regulation and accounting standards; credit rating agencies, executive pay; capital market supervision, and risk management.
- **Dealing with the impact on the real economy**. The policy instruments that can be employed to address the expected rise in unemployment and decline in economic growth are in the hands of the member states. Nevertheless, the EU can assist by adding short-term actions to its structural reform agenda, while investing in the future through: 1) increasing investment in R&D innovation and education; 2) promoting "flexicurity" [50] to protect and equip people rather than specific jobs; 3) freeing up businesses to build markets at home and internationally; and 4) enhancing competitiveness by promoting green technology, and overcoming energy security constraints and achieving environmental goals. In addition, the Commission will explore a wide range of ways in which EU members can increase their rate of economic growth.
- The impact of the financial crisis on the real economies of the EU members likely will require adjustments in the fiscal and monetary policies of the EU members. The Stability and Growth Pact [51] of the EU members should serve as the blueprint for members facing higher than expected levels of fiscal or monetary stimulus so that such policies should be accompanied by structural reforms. Such reforms should aim to sustain domestic demand in the short-run, ease transitions within and into the labor market, and increase potential growth by directing investment

into areas that will sustain employment and advance productivity. Reforms in the finance sector should focus on enhancing the competitive position of the European industry and finance the needs of small and medium-sized firms. The Commission will also attempt to counter an expected increase in unemployment by using funds provided under the European Social Fund [52] to reintroduce unemployed workers back into the work force.

- **A global response to the financial crisis**. The crisis has raised questions concerning global governance that are relative to the financial sector and to the need to maintain open trade markets. The EU intended to use the November 15, 2008 multi-nation economic summit In Washington D.C. to promote a series of measures to reform the global financial architecture. The Commission argued that the measures should include: 1) strengthening international regulatory standards; 2) strengthening international coordination among financial supervisors; 3) strengthening measures to monitor and coordinate macroeconomic policies; and 4) developing the capacity to address a financial crisis at the national regional and multilateral levels. Also, a financial architecture plan should include three key principles: 1) efficiency; 2) transparency and accountability; and 3) inclusion of representation from key emerging economies.

In concert with the European Framework for action, several European countries, including Germany, France, Italy, Austria, Netherlands, Portugal, Spain, and Norway announced plans to recapitalize banks and to provide government debt guarantees. European leaders agreed to increase the role of the IMF in preventing a future financial crisis, however, they could not agree on precisely what that role should be [53]. As a consequence, the leaders set a 100-day deadline to draw up reforms for the international financial system and asked the Bank for International Settlements (BIS) to develop a set of guidelines to ensure that banks hold enough capital to reduce the risks of a similar financial crisis.

On January 7, 2009, the BIS responded to the request by the G20 by publishing a first draft of its proposed guidelines [54] for "stress testing banks," or assessing the impact of various large shocks on the ability of banks to absorb losses. Stress testing is a risk management tool that is used by banks to assess the financial position of a bank under a severe but plausible scenario to absorb the impact of unexpected risks on the bank's capital position, which is comprised of common stock and retained earnings. Banks do not loan out their capital directly to borrowers, but use it as a cushion to help them absorb losses from loans and other banking activities. Currently, banks are required to engage in periodic stress testing as a risk management tool. The BIS guidelines provide a set of recommendations for bank supervisors as they review the conduct of stress tests within their banks in order to overcome shortcomings in the present system that failed to assess such risks as: the behavior of complex structured products; risks in relation to hedging strategies; pipeline or securitization risk; contingent risk; and funding liquidity risk.

"Bad Banks"

The United Kingdom, the Netherlands, Germany, and the European Central Bank are considering proposals to split off the bad assets of banks into a separate "bad bank" to prevent more banks from failing as did Sweden in the 1990s and Switzerland in 2008. The economic downturn is continuing to erode the value of the assets that banks are holding as capital, which is causing banks to curtail their lending and, in a growing number of cases, threatening the viability of the bank. The United Kingdom created such a bank when it took over Bradford & Bingley by selling off the healthy portion of the bank and holding "bad" assets. A hurdle that faces a bank with bad assets is that when the bank participates in such a bad asset program they are forced to lower the value they assign to their bad assets before they can move them to a bad bank, which further dilutes the value of the remaining shares of the bank and compounds the efforts by the bank to raise capital [55].

Germany is considering a plan that would shift bad assets from banks into special-purpose securities with government guarantees. Officials are also considering providing more generous accounting rules that would protect assets that experience a down grade in their value from having a negative impact on the value of the capital a bank uses to support its core business. In response to actions by Germany and the United Kingdom, the European Central Bank is drawing up guidelines for European governments that are considering establishing "bad" banks to forestall a competitive movement by EU governments. The ECB is also considering guidelines for some governments that are developing plans to guarantee the bad assets that remain on the books of banks to head off a move to gain a competitive advantage for some banks [56].

Phase IV: Fiscal Intervention

In the fourth phase, as the problems in credit markets persisted, the financial crisis spread to those activities in the real economy that are highly reliant on credit markets, and it reinforced concerns over the adequacy of capital provisions. Furthermore, the slowdown in economic growth weakened the capital position of financial institutions so that the financial crisis and the economic downturn have become negatively reinforcing. Governments have responded in this phase of the crisis by adopting macroeconomic stimulus measures to blunt the effects of the economic recession. In February 2008, Congress passed P.L. 110-185, the Economic Stimulus Act of 2008 to provide rebates to individuals on their income taxes in order to provide a fiscal boost to the U.S. economy [57]. Then in July 2008, Congress adopted, and President Bush signed, P.L. 110-289, the Housing and Economic Recovery Act of 2008 to provide an additional fiscal stimulus to the U.S. economy. In February 2009, as the U.S. economy continued to post large monthly losses in jobs, Congress adopted, and President Obama signed, a compromise measure of H.R. 1, the American Recovery and Reinvestment Act of 2009 to provide an additional fiscal stimulus to the U.S. economy. The British, French, and German governments also announced fiscal stimulus packages. Various central banks announced additional cuts in key interest rates as another effort to stimulate economic growth. On March 5, 2009, the European Central Bank and the Bank of England announced a cut in key interest rates by 0.5% to 1.5% and 0.5%, respectively, approaching the Federal Reserve rate of 0.25%. In addition, the Bank of England announced a quantitative easing in monetary policy, or increasing the money supply, by $150 billion over three months to stimulate economic growth [58].

European Economic Recovery Plan

On November 27, 2008, the European Commission proposed a $256 billion Economic Recovery Plan [59] that would fund cross-border projects, including investments in clean energy and upgraded telecommunications infrastructure. In all, the European Economic Recovery Plan is comprised of two parts. First, each EU member is asked to contribute an amount equivalent to 1.5% of their GDP to boost consumer demand. Second, members are tasked to invest in energy efficient equipment to create jobs and save energy, invest in environmentally clean technologies to convert such sectors as construction and automobiles to low-carbon sectors, and to invest in infrastructure and communications. The members of the European Council approved the plan in a meeting on December 12, 2008. As table 4 indicates, most European countries have announced some form of an economic stimulus package.

As part of the EC plan, budget rules imposed by the Stability and Growth Pact would be loosened to allow EU members to adopt economic stimulus plans to shore up their declining economic growth rates. The plan is intended to mesh with the goals and objectives outlined in the Lisbon Strategy to improve the rate of economic growth among EU members. This plan also proposes official support measures to increase the rate of employment and to focus investments on such high technology sectors as telecommunications and environmentally safe technologies. In addition to the proposed macroeconomic stimulus plan, various central banks have worked in concert to cut key interest rates in an effort to boost economic growth.

Germany

In an effort to confront worsening economic conditions, German Chancellor Angela Merkel proposed a package of stimulus measures, including spending for large-scale infrastructure projects, ranging from schools to communications. The stimulus package represents the second multi-billion euro fiscal stimulus package Germany has adopted in less than three months. The plan, announced on January13, 2009, reportedly was doubled from initial estimates to reach more than 60 billion Euros[60] (approximately $80 billion) over two years. The plan reportedly includes a pledge by Germany's largest companies to avoid mass job cuts in return for an increase in government subsidies for employees placed temporarily on short work weeks or on lower wages [61]. Other reports indicate that Germany is considering an emergency fund of up to 100 billion Euros in state-backed loans or guarantees to aid companies having problems getting credit [62].

Table 4. Recently Announced and Planned or Proposed Stimulus Packages

Date Announced	Country	$Billion	Status, Package Contents
12-Dec-08	European Union	256.00	Fund cross-border projects including clean energy and upgraded telecommunications architecture. Each EU member to contribute an amount equivalent to 1.5% of GDP to boost consumer spending. M asked to boost spending in energy efficient equipment and clean technologies.
13-Jan-09	Germany	65.00	Infrastructure, tax cuts, child bonus, increase in some social benefits, $3,250 incentive for trading in cars more than nine years old for a new or slightly used car.
24-Nov-08	United Kingdom	29.60	Proposed plan includes a 2.5% cut in the value added tax for 13 months, a postponement of corporate tax increases, government guarantees for loans to small and midsize businesses, spending on public works, including public housing and energy efficiency. Plan includes an increase in income taxes on those making more than $225,000 and increase National Insurance contribution for all but the lowest income workers.
5-Nov-08	France	33.00	Public sector investments (road and rail construction, refurbishment and improving ports and river infrastructure, building and renovating universities, research centers, prisons, courts, and monuments) and loans for carmakers. Does not include the previously planned $15 billion in credits and tax breaks on investments by companies in 2009.
16-Nov-08	Italy	52.00	Awaiting final parliamentary approval. Three year program. Measures to spur consumer credit, provide loans to companies, and rebuild infrastructure. February 6, announced a $2.56 billion stimulus package that was part of the three-year program that includes payments of up to $1,950 for trading in an old car for a new, less polluting one and 20% tax deductions for purchases of appliances and furniture.
22-Nov-08	Netherlands	7.50	Tax deduction to companies that make large investments, funds to companies that hire temporary workers, and creation of a program to find jobs for the unemployed.

Table 4. (Continued).

Date Announced	Country	$Billion	Status, Package Contents
11-Dec-08	Belgium	2.60	Increase in unemployment benefits, lowering of the value added tax on construction, abolishing taxes on energy, energy checks for families, faster payments of invoices by the government, faster government investment in railroads and buildings, and lowering of employer's fiscal contributions.
27-Nov-08	Spain	14.30	Public works, help for automobile industry, environmental projects, research and development, restoring residential and military housing, and funds to support the sick.
14-Jan-09	Portugal	2.89	Funds to be provided to medium and small-sized businesses, money for infrastructure, particularly schools, and investment in technological improvement.
20-Nov-08	Israel	5.40	Public works to include desalination plants, doubling railway routes, adding R&D funding, increasing export credits, cutting assorted taxes, and aid packages for employers to hire new workers.
21-Dec-08	Switzerland	0.59	Public works spending on flood defense, natural disaster and energy-efficiency projects.
5-Dec-08	Sweden	2.70	Public infrastructure and investment in human capital, including job training, vocational workshops, and workplace restructuring.; extension of social benefits to part-time workers.
26-Jan-09	Norway	2.88	Investment in construction, infrastructure, and renovation of state-owned buildings, tax breaks for companies.

Source: Various news articles.

Notes: Amounts are in U.S. dollars. Currency conversions to U.S. dollars were done in the news articles or by using current exchange rates.

Chancellor Merkel has been criticized within her own government and by other leaders in Europe for not moving aggressively enough to address either the financial crisis, or the economic downturn [63]. Initially, Merkel attempted to block and then offered tepid support for the EU plan to provide an EU-wide economic package to stimulate growth. Chancellor Merkel indicated that she has a fundamental disagreement over the effectiveness of such macroeconomic stimulus measures especially given the protracted struggle in Germany to reduce its government deficit spending to meet the guidelines in the EU Stability and Growth Pact. Instead, Merkel has argued in favor of targeted actions taken independently by EU members to tackle their own unique set of circumstances. Some observers argue that such a plan could come at a high political cost to Merkel, who vowed when she was elected to balance Germany's government budget by 2011.

Overall, Germany's response to the economic downturn changed markedly between December 2008 and January 2009 as economic conditions continued to worsen. In a December 2008 article, German Finance Minister Peer Steinbruck defended Germany's approach at the time. According to Steinbruck, Germany disagreed with the EU plan to provide a broad economic stimulus plan, because it favored an approach that is more closely tailored to the German economy. He argued that Germany is providing a counter-cyclical stimulus program even though it is contrary to its long-term goal of reducing its government budget deficit. Important to this program, however, are such "automatic stabilizers" as unemployment benefits that automatically increase without government action since such benefits play a larger role in the German economy than in other economies. Steinbruck argued that, "our experience since the 1970s has shown that...stimulus programs fail to achieve the desired effect...It is more likely that such large-scale stimulus programs – and tax cuts as well – would not have any effects in real time. It is unclear whether general tax cuts can significantly encourage consumption during a recession, when many consumers are worried about losing their jobs. The history of the savings rate in Germany points to the opposite"[64].

France

France, which has been leading efforts to develop a coordinated European response to the financial crisis, has proposed a package of measures estimated to cost over $500 billion. The French government is creating two state agencies that will provide funds to sectors where they are needed. One entity will issue up to

$480 billion in guarantees on inter-bank lending issued before December 31, 2009, and would be valid for five years. The other entity will use a $60 billion fund to recapitalize struggling companies by allowing the government to buy stakes in the firms. On January 16, 2009, President Sarkozy announced that the French government would take a tougher stance toward French banks that seek state aid. Up to that point, France had injected $15 billion in the French banking system. In order to get additional aid, banks would be required to suspend dividend payments to shareholders and bonuses to top management and to increase credit lines to such clients as exporters. France reportedly was preparing to inject more money into the banking system [65].

On December 4, 2008, President Sarkozy announced a $33 billion (26 billion euros) package of stimulus measures to accelerate planned public investments [66]. The package is focused primarily on infrastructure projects and investments by state-controlled firms, including a canal north of Paris, renovation of university buildings, new metro cars, and construction of 70,000 new homes, in addition to 30,000 unfinished homes the government has committed to buy in 2009. The plan also includes a 200 Euro payment to low-income households. On December 15, 2008, France agreed to provide the finance division of Renault and Peugeot $1.2 billion in credit guarantees and an additional $250 million to support the car manufacturers' consumer finance division [67]. In an interview on French TV on January 14, 2009, French Prime Minister Francois Fillon indicated that the French government is considering an increase in aid to the French auto industry, including Renault and Peugeot [68]. The auto industry and its suppliers reportedly employ about 10% of France's labor force.

United Kingdom

On November 24, 2008, Britain's majority Labor party presented a plan to Parliament to stimulate the nation's slowing economy by providing a range of tax cuts and government spending projects totaling 20 billion pounds (about $30 billion) [69]. The stimulus package includes a 2.5% cut in the value added tax (VAT), or sales tax, for 13 months, a postponement of corporate tax increases, and government guarantees for loans to small and midsize businesses. The plan also includes government plans to spend 4.5 billion pounds on public works, such as public housing and energy efficiency. Some estimates indicate that the additional spending required by the plan will push Britain's government budget deficit in 2009 to an amount equivalent to 8% of GDP. To pay for the plan, the government would increase income taxes on those making more than 150,000 pounds (about $225,000) from 40% to 45% starting in April 2011. In addition, the British plan would increase the National Insurance contributions for all but the lowest income workers [70].

On January 14, 2009, British Business Secretary Lord Mandelson unveiled an additional package of measures by the Labor government to provide credit to small and medium businesses that have been hard pressed for credit as foreign financial firms have reduced their level of activity in the UK. The three measures are: 1) a 10 billion pound (approximately $14 billion) Capital Working Scheme to provide banks with guarantees to cover 50% of the risk on existing and new working capital loans on condition that the banks must use money freed up by the guarantee to make new loans; 2) a one billion pound Enterprise Finance Guarantee Scheme to assist small, credit-worthy companies by providing guarantees to banks of up to 75% of loans to small businesses; and 3) a 75 million pound Capital for Enterprise Fund to convert debt to equity for small businesses [71].

Prime Minister Brown has come under sharp criticism from abroad over the stimulus packages and from opposition party leaders at home over his handling of the economy before and during the financial crisis. He is also being criticized over the depreciating pound and the lack of evidence that the British economy is showing signs of responding to the economic rescue plan. German Finance Minister Peer Steinbruck, for one, called the British plan, "crass Keynesianism." [72] At home, the depreciating pound has undermined the credibility of Prime Minister Brown who previously had equated a weak currency with a weak economy and a weak government [73]. Depreciation in the exchange value of the pound puts upward pressure on domestic prices as a result of higher import prices, but it helps boost exports by reducing the cost of British goods in foreign markets.

OUTLOOK

The financial crisis has underscored the growing interdependence between financial centers and has tested the ability of EU members to cooperate in developing an EU-wide response. The financial interdependence between the United States and the European Union means that the EU and the United States share common concerns over the global impact of the financial crisis and the economic downturn. It also means that they both support and hope to benefit from efforts by national governments to stimulate their economies. Such stimulus measures, however, could become a source of friction if some of the larger economies are viewed as not carrying their share of the burden for a global recovery by providing stimulus measures that are commensurate with the size of their economy. The EU and the United States also share common concerns over the stability of East European countries. These common concerns may eventually work to spur EU members to forge a common consensus regarding the necessity of providing financial assistance to East European countries, but some observers are concerned that such a consensus may come too late to forestall serious economic deterioration in the East European economies, with implications for negative effects on the economies in Europe and the United States.

In addition to these concerns, the United States and the EU members are share common concerns over the organization of financial markets domestically and abroad and seek to improve supervision and regulation of individual institutions and of international markets. Extensive cross- border banking activities by a number of EU countries has demonstrated that serious problems in one country can have a substantial impact on the financial system elsewhere, while governments may face potentially large liabilities that are associated with branches in another country [74]. One solution that is being considered is in developing the organizational structures within national economies that can provide oversight of the different segments of the highly complex financial system. Such oversight is viewed by many as critical, because financial markets are generally considered to play an indispensible role in allocating capital and facilitating economic activity. Some observers argue, however, that the complexity of the financial system has outstripped the ability of national regulators to oversee effectively.

The financial crisis also has revealed extensive interdependency across financial market segments both within many of the advanced national financial markets and across national borders. As a result, the United States and members of the EU share mutual interests in solving both the financial crisis and the economic recession, because the two crises have become negatively reinforcing events. EU leaders are also especially concerned over the impact the economic crisis is having on the political stability and commitment to market reforms among the emerging economies of Eastern Europe. EU leaders are supporting a number of efforts to provide assistance to European economies, but they may have to expend considerably more resources if the economic crisis persists for an extended period of time.

The international nature of financial markets and capital flows likely means that efforts to address the current situation and to prevent future crisis require a coordinated response between the United States and the EU. A coordinated response likely will need to address such issues as financial market regulation, oversight of financial firms and institutions, greater transparency, and the role of independent credit rating and auditing institutions. Significant differences remain, however, among EU members and between some EU members and the United States over issues of financial supervision and regulation that could significantly complicate future efforts to craft a coordinated approach to supervising financial market at an international level. Some EU members favor a strong central authority that can monitor financial markets, while others favor strong national authorities with a weaker role for an international body. EU members recognize that economic integration means that financial and economic crises can spill across national borders, but their efforts to implement a coordinated response are being hampered by very real differences in the impact the economic recession is having on individual EU members.

The financial crisis also raises important questions about how a nation can protect its depositors from financial crisis elsewhere and about the level of financial sector debt that is manageable without risking system-wide failure. In addition, the failure of a number of large banks raises questions about bank supervision, primarily about how national governments should supervise foreign financial firms that are operating within their borders. This issue raises questions about how countries can protect their depositors when foreign-owned firms attempt to withdraw deposits from one market in order to offset losses in another. One approach focuses on broad levels of cooperation between national governments with each government addressing the crisis from its own perspective and in its own limited way. For a number of governments in Europe this approach is appealing, because their economies and their banks have felt little direct effect from the crisis.

An alternative approach argues in favor of a more integrated and coordinated response from national governments and central banks. This approach argues that a coordinated systemic approach is necessary, because financial markets in the United States and Europe have become highly integrated as a result of cross-border investment by banks, securities brokers, and other financial firms. As a result of this integration, economic and financial developments that affect national economies are difficult to contain and are quickly transmitted across national borders, as attested to by the financial crisis of 2008. As financial firms react to a financial crisis in one area, their actions can spill over to other areas as they withdraw assets from foreign markets to shore up their domestic operations. For instance, as Icelandic banks began to default, Britain used an anti-terrorism law to seize the deposits of the banks to prevent the banks from shifting funds from Britain to Iceland [75]. Banks and financial firms in Europe have felt the repercussions of the U.S. financial crisis as U.S. firms operating in Europe and as

ial Services Committee. This committee is composed of ntatives of the ministries of finance and the European Commission cusses and provides guidance on cross-sector strategic and policy

ea countries initially sketched out a broad response to the financial n, their response to bank foreclosures and to subsequent issues has ized by some as somewhat disjointed. The financial crisis and turn have exposed deep fissures within the EU and even within the tries over the policy course to follow. As a first response to the EU governments and their central banks focused policy initiatives redit markets that there was an availability of credit and liquidity, terest rates, and by providing foreign currency, primarily dollars, cy arrangements. In addition to continuing efforts to restore the ets, EU members also face a worsening economic climate that s by individual central banks, international organizations, and ions by EU members and other governments.

ervices Directive

as adopted a number of directives that provide a basic framework rs to coordinate financial regulation across the EU and to integrate rs. One such directive is the Investment Services Directive (ISD) to force on January 1, 1996. The ISD provided general principles curities regulations, with the goal of providing mutual recognition across the EU [78]. The ISD created a "European Passport" that cross-border right of establishment for non-bank investment firms m to provide services across borders for investment firms to carry ange of investment business. Under the passport, firms were d supervised by domestic authorities, but could still provide stment services in other EU countries. Such cross-border services cting and executing buy and sell orders on an agency basis, dealing, underwriting portfolios, and such additional services as providing lvice, advising on mergers and acquisitions, safekeeping and of securities, and foreign exchange transactions.

pean "passport" provision required member states to dismantle islation that prevented cross-border branching and freedom of ertheless, EU members retained the responsibility for determining

European firms operating in the United States have adjusted their operations in response to the crisis.

The financial crisis also raises questions about the cost and benefits of branch banking across national borders where banks can grow to be so large that disruptions in the financial market can cause defaults that outstrip the resources of national central banks to address. Such branch banking across national borders has significantly expanded financial opportunities for individual investors and firms alike and is unlikely to disappear as a result of the current financial crisis. Nevertheless, if some financial institutions are deemed to be too big to fail, financial regulators and national governments likely will need to address the issue of who and how such institutions should be supervised when their operations span national borders and they are engaged in a vast array of banking and investment operations.

The European Economic Recovery Plan calls for EU members to contribute an amount equal to 1.5% of their respective GDP to stimulate economic growth. Some observers argue, however, that the size of an economic stimulus package should be sufficient to address the size and nature of the relevant economic crisis, instead of being determined as a certain percentage of GDP. The nature of the current economic recession may well call for a larger stimulus package than that dictated by a pre-set percentage of a country's GDP. The ability of individual countries to provide a large economic stimulus, however, may be inhibited by actions they already have taken and by concerns over providing the right balance between sometimes competing goals of implementing policies that have a large and lasting impact but that do not threaten the long-term stability in national finances.

So far, members of the EuropeanUnion have struggled to implement a coordinated response to the economic crises. In the current context, many argue that an export-led recovery strategy is not an option. Efforts to promote exports or to discourage imports likely will not provide a significant boost to economic growth in any one country and could lead to retaliation by other countries depending on the costs and benefits of implementing such a strategy. The slowdown in economic activity has reduced exports world-wide and banks are balking at providing trade financing to small and medium firms [76]. The financial crisis also has weakened some of the traditional mechanisms through which monetary policy is transmitted. A number of EU countries already have used monetary expansion and cuts in interest rates to provide liquidity during the financial crisis and may have limited ability to provide for additional fiscal measures to stimulate their economies. Furthermore, some EU members disagree over how best to implement a coordinated economic stimulus plan, due in part to deep philosophical differences among EU members over the conduct of macroeconomic policies.

Another important factor that is affecting the EU's response to the economic recession is the need to develop new policies in a manner that meshes with the carefully crafted and highly negotiated Directives that already exist within the EU framework. These Directives act as guiding principles for EU members. In particular, the call for economic stimulus has created a conflict for some EU Members who are politically and philosophically committed to the goals of the Growth and Stability Pact and with the development goals of the Lisbon Strategy. Arguably, these agreements have helped stabilize economic conditions in Europe by bringing down the overall rate of price inflation and by reducing government budget deficits. In addition to the Lisbon Strategy, EU members likely will consider proposals to examine financial supervision and regulation within the context of the EU's Directive on Financial Services and the Financial Services Action Plan (FSAP) when it engages in negotiations with the United States and the G20 later in 2009.

APPENDIX A. OVERVIEW OF THE EUROPEAN UNION

The European Union is a political and economic union of 27 member states, formally established in 1993 by the Treaty of Maastricht out of existing structures that had evolved in steps since the 1950s. The EU has worked to develop a single economic market through a standardized system of laws which apply across all member states and which provide the freedom of movement of people, goods, services and capital. This process of economic integration is complicated by a dual system that gives the members of the EU significant independence within the EU and broad discretion to interpret and implement EU directives. The EU maintains common trade, agricultural, and fisheries policies, and a regional development policy. EU economic integration is compounded further by sixteen member states, collectively known as the Eurozone [77], which have adopted the euro as a common currency and operate as a bloc within the EU. Major institutions and bodies of the EU include: the European Commission, the European Parliament, the Council of the European Union, the European Council, the European Court of Justice, and the European Central Bank (ECB). Through various Directives, the EU has moved to increase financial integration within the Union to make the monetary union represented by the Eurozone operate more efficiently and the help the EU members realize the full potential of the EU.

Within the EU, the European Commissi
and is responsible for proposing legislation
the Union's treaties, and the general day-
Commission operates as a cabinet governme
member. One of the 27 is the Commissio
Barroso) appointed by the European Counci
Parliament, for a term of five years. Rela
process provides for each member to ha
framework, which complicates efforts to coo
EU, there are a number of bodies that bri
ministers, and central bankers of the EU me
the Economic and Financial Affairs Council
with the Council. ECOFIN's responsi
coordination, economic surveillance, monito
of the EU's budget. The key bodies in
following:

- **European Banking Committe**
representatives of the ministries c
advises the EU Commission on poli
and on proposals in the banking are
- **Committee of European Banki**
comprised of representatives of sup
and coordinates on regulatory and s
- **European Central Bank**. The ECB
monitoring in cooperation with na
agencies.
- **Banking Supervision Committe**
national central banks, banking sup
monitors and assesses development
of regulatory and supervisory requi
and it promotes cooperation and exc
banks and supervisory authorities o
- **Economic and Financial Con**
representatives of ministries of fin
ECB, and central banks to p
developments in financial markets.
- **Financial Stability Table**. This
financial stability issues.

- **Fi**
re
an
iss

The eu
crisis. Sinc
been chara
economic d
euro area c
financial cr
on reassuri
by reducing
through cu
financial m
requires ac
coordinated

Investme

The EU
for EU men
financial se
that entered
for national
of regulatio
provided fo
and the free
out a wide
authorized
specified in
included: co
managing a
investment
administrati
The Eu
restrictive l
services. Ne

their own domestic laws and regulations concerning such issues as fitness, authorization, capital requirements, and protection of client assets. EU members could also impose rules and regulations on investment firms using the European passport as long as the rules and regulations were, "in the interest of the general good," and applied to the business activities that the firms carried out in their state. The ISD opened up stock exchange membership in all member states to all types of investment firms, whether bank or non- bank entities. Another objective of the ISD was to eliminate the so-called concentration rule in order to allow member states that lacked their own securities trading floor to access electronic terminals with investment firms and banks in other member states, thereby allowing them to be members of the markets on a remote electronic basis.

Financial Services Action Plan

In 1999, the EU replaced the Investment Services Directive with the Financial Services Action Plan. The Plan consists of a set of measures that are intended to remove the remaining formal barriers in financial markets among EU members and to provide a legal and regulatory environment that supports the integration of EU financial markets [79]. Similar to the ISD, the FSAP process supports a two-pronged approach that combines EU directives with national laws. The EU directives provide for a general level of regulation concerning the provision of financial services across borders and the harmonization of national regulations governing cross-border activities. EU members, however, retain the right to regulate firms within their own borders, as long as those firms, whether foreign or domestic, are treated equally. The FSAP contains 42 articles, 38 of which were implemented, that are intended to meet three specific objectives: 1) a single wholesale market; 2) an open and secure retail market; and 3) state-of-the art rules and supervision. Wholesale measures relate to securities issuance and trading; securities settlement; accounts; and corporate restructuring. Retail measures relate to insurance; savings through pension funds and mutual funds; retail payments; electronic money; and money laundering.

Markets in Financial Instruments Directive

The cornerstone of the FSAP's achievement is the Markets in Financial Instruments Directive (MiFID), which became effective on November 1, 2007. The MiFID establishes a comprehensive, harmonized set of rules for Europe's securities markets so financial services firms can provide investment services in each of the EU member states. MiFID retained the principles of the EU "passport" and extended the list of services and financial instruments that are covered by the passport procedures, including investment advice. MiFID also removed the so-called concentration rule that required investment firms to route all stock transactions through established exchanges.

MiFID introduced the concept of 'maximum harmonization' which places more emphasis on home state supervision. This is a change from the previous EU financial service legislation which featured a "minimum harmonization and mutual recognition" concept. Minimum harmonization provides for a law or a regulation that sets a floor, or a minimum standard, that EU countries were expected to meet in developing legislation. Maximum harmonization provides for a maximum level of a law or a regulation that sets the maximum allowable standard that can be adopted in domestic laws or regulations. At times some EU members have been accused of adopting domestic measures that exceed the EU standard in a manner that acted as a protectionist barrier.

Some key elements of the MiFID are:

- Authorization, regulation and passporting. Firms covered by MiFID are authorized and regulated in their "home state." Once a firm is authorized, it can use the MiFID passport to provide services to customers in other EU member states. These services are regulated by the "home state" in which the firm is authorized.
- Client categorization. MiFID requires firms to categorize clients as "eligible counter-parties," professional clients, or retail clients, with increasing levels of protection.
- Client order handling. MiFID places requirements on information that needs to be captured when firms accept client orders in order to ensure that a firm is acting in a client's best interests.
- Pre-trade transparency. MiFID requires the operators of various kinds of equity exchanges to make the best bid and offer prices available to potential buyers and sellers.
- Post-trade transparency. MiFID requires firms to publish the price, volume and time of all trades in listed shares, even if executed outside of a regulated market, unless certain requirements are met to allow for deferred publication.
- Best execution. MiFID will require that firms take all reasonable steps to obtain the best possible result in the execution of an order for a client. The best possible result is not limited to execution price but also includes

cost, speed, likelihood of execution and likelihood of settlement and any other factors deemed relevant.

- Systematic Internalizer. A Systematic Internalizer is a firm that executes orders from its clients against its own book or against orders from other clients and are treated as mini-exchanges, which makes them subject to pre-trade and post-trade transparency requirements

Capital Requirements Directive

The Capital Requirements Directive, which became effective in January 2007, introduced a supervisory framework within the EU for investment management firms and banks. The purpose of the Directive is to move the EU towards complying with the Basel II[80] rules on capital measurement, adequacy, and related market disclosure disciplines. This Directive promotes a risk based capital management methodology through a "three pillar" structure that includes: 1) new standards that set out the minimum capital requirements that firms will be required to meet for credit, market, and operational risk; 2) firms and supervisors will be required to decide whether they are holding enough capital to address the risks realized under Pillar I and act accordingly; and 3) improve market discipline by requiring firms to publish certain details about their risks, capital, and risk management. The Directive also requires firms to make provision for a charge against their capital for operational risks in order to identify, monitor, manage, and report on certain types of external events that may have a negative effect on their capital. The Directive applies not only to internationally active banks, which is the main focus of the Basel II approach, but it also applies to all credit institutions and investment firms irrespective of the size, scope of activities, or levels of sophistication. Under the Directive, firms are required to meet rules governing the minimum amounts of their own financial resources they must have in order to cover the risks to which they may be exposed.

Lamfalussy Process

As the European Commission crafted a coordinated EU approach to the financial crisis, it has done so in accordance with a set of procedures known as the Lamfalussy Process. The Lamfalussy structure provides a framework for updating EU financial regulations and developing similar supervisory practices. While this process can be time consuming, it provides a process for EU members to follow so that policies that are considered through the process ultimately will be acceptable to all EU members and, therefore, will be more likely to be implemented. MiFID is the most significant piece of legislation that has been introduced under this process. Originally developed in March of 2001, it is named after the chair of the EU advisory committee that created it, Alexandre Lamfalussy. The process is composed of four "levels," each focusing on a specific stage of the implementation of legislation. Level 1 is traditional EU decision making, which means that decisions are adopted in the form of Directives or Regulations proposed by the Commission and then approved under the co-decision procedure by the European Parliament and the EU Council. Legislation adopted at this level primarily establishes the core values of a law.

At the second level, sector-specific committees and regulators provide advice on developing the technical details of the principles that were adopted in Level 1 and then bring the measure to a vote by the representatives of each EU member. These measures can be adopted, adapted and updated by the Commission after they have been submitted to the European Securities Committee (ES C), a committee composed mainly of members of Ministries of Finance, and to the European Parliament for their opinion. The Committee of European Securities Regulators (CESR), an independent advisory body made up of securities regulators, also advises the Commission on the technical implementing details to be included in Level 2 legislation. This advice is provided in response to specific "mandates" from the Commission asking for help in particular areas. Level 2 implementing measures do not alter the principles agreed upon at Level 1, but simply provide the technical details that are necessary in order to make the principles operational.

At the third level, national regulators work on coordinating new regulations with other nations. At this stage, CESR may adopt non-binding guidelines or common standards regarding matters not covered by EU legislation, as long as these standards are compatible with the legislation adopted at Level 1 and Level 2.

The fourth level involves compliance and enforcement of the new rules and laws, including initiating proceedings on cases of non-conformity.

The Lamfalussy Process is intended to provide several benefits over traditional lawmaking, including more-consistent interpretation, convergence in national supervisory practices, and a general boost in the quality of legislation on financial services. Nevertheless, the Lamfalussy Process has sparked controversy, because some critics argue that the procedure can effectively bypass accountable oversight by the European Council and the elected European Parliament, thereby embodying a move away from representative democracy towards technocratic and participatory democracy.

REFERENCES

[1] Members of the European Union are: Austria, Belgium, Bulgaria, Cyprus, the Czech Republic, Denmark, Estonia, Finland, France, Germany, Greece, Hungary, Ireland, Italy, Latvia, Lithuania, Luxembourg, Malta, the Netherlands, Poland, Portugal, Romania, Slovakia, Slovenia, Spain, Sweden, and the United Kingdom.

[2] Blair, Dennis C., Annual Threat Assessment of the Intelligence Community for the Senate Select Committee on Intelligence, February 12, 2009.

[3] Members of the Euro area have adopted the Euro as their common currency. Member countries are: Austria, Belgium, Cyprus, Finland, France, Germany, Greece, Ireland, Italy, Luxembourg, Malta, the Netherlands, Portugal, Slovakia, Slovenia, and Spain.

[4] Pan, Phillip P., Economic Crisis Fuels Unrest in E. Europe, *The Washington Post*, January 26, 2009, p, A1.

[5] Shin, Annys, World Bank to Offer Aid to Eastern Europe, *The Washington Post*, February 27, 2009, p. A10.

[6] To join the Eurozone, countries must keep their government budget deficits, their overall level of government debt, and the rate of price inflation below specified fixed ceilings and hold their currencies within a preset range to the Euro for two years.

[7] Forelle, Charles, EU Rejects a Rescue of Faltering East Europe, *The Wall Street Journal*, March 2, 2009.

[8] Bryant, Chris, EU Leaders Push Sweeping Regulations, *Financial Times*, February 22, 2009.

[9] *EU Banking Structures*, European Central Bank, October 2008.

[10] The Stability and Growth Pact (SGP) is an agreement by European Union members to conduct their fiscal policy in a manner that facilitates and maintains the Economic and Monetary Union of the European Union. The Pact was adopted in 1997 and is based on Articles 99 and 104 of the European Community Treaty, or the Maastricht Treaty, and related decisions. It consists of monitoring the fiscal policies of the members by the European Commission and the Council so that fiscal discipline is maintained and enforced in the Economic and Monetary Union (EMU). The actual criteria that members states must respect are: 1) an annual budget deficit no higher than 3% of GDP, and 2) a national debt lower than 60% of GDP, or approaching that value.

[11] The Lisbon Strategy for Growth and Jobs is a plan adopted by EU members to improve economic growth and employment among the EU members by becoming the most competitive knowledge based economy in the world by 2010. The comprehensive strategy includes adopting sustainable macroeconomic policies, business friendly regulatory and tax policies and benefits, improved education and training, and greater investment in energy efficient and environmentally friendly technology. Two major goals include total public and private investment of 3% of Europe's GDP in research and employment by 2010, and an employment rate of 70% by the same date. A comprehensive report on the Lisbon Strategy is available at: http://ec.europa.EU/ growthand jobs/pdf/kok_report_en.pdf.

[12] The Financial Services Action Plan replaced the Investment Services Directive and contains a set of measures that are intended to remove the remaining formal barriers in the financial services market among EU members and to provide a legal and regulatory environment that supports the integration of the EU financial markets. *The EU Financial Services Action Plan: A Guide*, HM Treasury, the Financial Services authority, and the Bank of England, July 31, 2003.

[13] **Flash Estimates for the Fourth Quarter of 2008, Eurostat news release, STAT/09/19, February 13, 2009.**

[14] See CRS Report R40173, *Causes of the Financial Crisis*, by Mark Jickling; CRS Report R40007, *Financial Market Turmoil and U.S. Macroeconomic Performance*, by Craig K. Elwell; CRS Report RL34412, *Containing Financial Crisis*, by Mark Jickling; CRS Report RS22963, *Financial Market Intervention*, by Edward V. Murphy and Baird Webel; and CRS Report RL34742, *The Global Financial and Economic Crisis: Analysis and Policy Implications*, coordinated by Dick K. Nanto.

[15] Fender, Ingo, and Jacob Gyntelberg, Overview: Global Financial Crisis Spurs Unprecedented Policy Actions, *BIS Quarterly Review*, Bank for International Settlements, December 2008.

[16] *Regional Economic Outlook: Europe*, International Monetary Fund, April, 2008, p. 19-20; and *EU Banking Structures*, European Central Bank, October 2008, p. 26.

[17] Commercial paper is a short-term unsecured money market security with a fixed maturity issued by large banks and corporations to get money to meet short-term debt obligations and is only backed by an issuing bank or corporation's promise to pay the face amount on the maturity date. Asset-backed commercial paper is a form of commercial paper that is collateralized by other financial assets.

[18] CRS ReportRS22988, *Iceland's Financial Crisis*, by James K. Jackson.

[19] Anderson, Camilla, Iceland Gets Help to Recover From Historic Crisis, *IMF Survey Magazine*, November 19, 2008.

[20] Credit default swaps are insurance-like contracts that promise to cover losses on certain securities in the event of a default. They typically apply to municipal bonds, corporate debt and mortgage securities and are sold by banks, hedge funds, and others. The buyer of the credit default insurance pays premiums over a period of time in return for peace of mind, knowing that losses will be covered if a default happens. They are supposed to work similarly to someone taking out home insurance to protect against losses from fire and theft.

[21] *Regional Economic Outlook: Europe*, International Monetary Fund, November, 2007, p. 6.; and *Quarterly Review*, Bank for International Settlements, December, 2008. p. 4.

[22] Chailloux, Alexandre, Simon Gray, Ulrich Kluh, Seiichi Shimizu, and Peter Stella, *Central Bank Response to the 2007-08 Financial Market Turbulence: Experiences and Lessons Drawn.* IMF Working Paper wP/08/210, International Monetary Fund, September 2008.

[23] Bernanke, Ben S., Liquidity Provision by the Federal Reserve, May 13, 2008.

[24] 2Borio, Claudio, and William Nelson, Monetary Operations and the Financial Crisis, *Quarterly Review*, March 2008, Bank for International Settlements.

[25] The Special Liquidity Scheme was launched by the Bank of England on April 21, 2008, to allow banks to temporarily swap their high-quality mortgage-backed and other securities for UK Treasury bills. A number of features of the program are: the swap of government securities will be for one year, but renewable at the Bank of England's discretion for up to three years; the Treasury securities will be available with a fee based on the spread between the LIBOR (the London Interbank Offer Rate) rate and the rate on certain government bonds; risks on the mortgage securities remains with the banks and the banks are required to use only rated assets as collateral; the swaps are available only for assets that were on the bank's balance sheets at the end of 2007 and cannot be used to finance new lending, and the assets of the banks are subject to valuation by the Bank of England; securities provided by the Bank of England are to be marketable Treasury securities that the banks can choose to hold, use as part of the Bank of England's standard market operations, or swap them for cash; the scheme will be closed down by October 2011 with all Treasury securities

returned to the Bank of England; and the scheme will not be independent of the Bank of England's monetary policy actions.

[26] *Financial Stability Report*, April 2008, Bank of England. P. 10

[27] Ibid., p. 31.

[28] Summit of the Euro Area Countries: Declaration on a Concerted European Action Plan of the Euro Area Countries, European Union, October 12, 2008.

[29] EU Sets up Crisis Unit to Boost Financial Oversight, Thompson Financial News, October 16, 2008.

[30] Ibid.

[31] Bradbury, Adam, EU Eyes Next Step on Clearing *The Wall Street Journal Europe*, January 7, 2009. P. 21.

[32] Hilsenrath, Jon, Joellen Perry, and Sudeep Reddy, Central Banks Launch Coordinated Attack; Emergency Rate Cuts Fail to Halt stock Slide; U.S. Treasury Considers Buying Stakes in Banks as Direct Move to Shore Up Capital, *The Wall Street Journal*, October 8, 2008, p. A1.

[33] The original eight banks are: Bank of America, Bank of New York Mellon Corporation, Citigroup Incorporated, Goldman Sachs Group Incorporated, JPMorgan Chase & Company, Morgan Stanley, State Street Corporation, and Wells Fargo and Company. Since this initial injection, nearly 50 banks have participated in the Capital Purchase Program.

[34] Hilsenrath, Jon, Joellen Perry, and Liz Rappaport, Fed Steps up Assault on Slump; U.S. is Joined in Rate Cuts by China, Norway; Doubts Linger on Easing's Impact, *The Wall Street Journal*, October 30, 2008, p. A1.

[35] Atkins, Ralph, and Chris Giles, Deep Rate Cuts in Europe, *Financial Times*, November 7, 2008, p. 1.

[36] Atkins, Ralph, ECB Acts and Hints at More to Come Soon, *Financial Times*, November 7, 2008, p. 2.

[37] *78th Annual Report*, Bank for International Settlements, p. 104-105.

[38] The central banks include: Swiss National Bank, European Central Bank, Bank of England, Bank of Japan, Bank of Canada, Reserve Bank of Australia, Sveriges Riksbank (Sweden), National Bank of Denmark, Central Bank of Norway, Reserve Bank of Norway, Reserve Bank of New Zealand, Central Bank of Brazil, Bank of Mexico, Bank of Korea, Monetary Authority of Singapore, Swiss National Bank, and National Bank of Poland.

[39] The G-7 is comprised of Canada, France, Germany, Italy, Japan, the United Kingdom, and the United States.

[40] *G-7 Finance Ministers and Central Bank Governors Plan of Action*, press release HP- 1195, October 10, 2008, United States Department of the Treasury.

[41] Summit of the Euro Area Countries: Declaration on a Concerted European Action Plan of the Euro Area Countries, European Union, October 12, 2008

[42] Perry, Joellen, and Marcus Walker, Europe's Central Banks Deliver Sweeping Rate Cuts, *Financial Times*, December 5, 2008. P. 1.

[43] Bank of England Reduces Bank Rate by 0.5 Percentage Points to 1.5%, Bank of England news release, January 8, 2009.

[44] Bank of England Reduces Bank Rate by 0.5 Percentage Points to 1.0%, Bank of England news release, February 5, 2009.

[45] Perry, Joellen, Nicholas Winning, and Joe Parkinson, Euro-Zone Activity Slows – Large ECB Rate Cut Expected After Data on Inflation, Services, *The Wall Street Journal Europe*, January 7, 2009. P. 2; Statement by Jean-Claude Trichet, European Central Bank, January15, 2009.

[46] Statement by Jean-Claude Trichet.

[47] The TARP funds have been used instead to inject capital directly into banks through purchases of newly-issued preferred stock.

[48] *Financial Stability Plan Fact Sheet*, U.S. Department of the Treasury, news release, February 9, 2009.

[49] *From Financial Crisis to Recovery: A European Framework for Action*, Communication From the Commission, European Commission, COM(2008) 706 final, October 29, 2008.

[50] The combination of labor market flexibility and security for workers.

[51] The Stability and Growth Pact (SGP) is an agreement by European Union members to conduct their fiscal policy in a manner that facilitates and maintains the Economic and Monetary Union of the European Union. The Pact was adopted in 1997 and is based on Articles 99 and 104 of the European Community Treaty, or the Maastricht Treaty, and related decisions. It consists of monitoring the fiscal policies of the members by the European Commission and the Council so that fiscal discipline is maintained and enforced in the European Monetary Union (EMU). The actual criteria that member states must respect are 1) an annual budget deficit no higher than 3% of GDP , and 2) a national debt lower than 60% of GDP or approaching that value.

[52] The European Social Fund, created in 1957, is the EU's main financial instrument for assisting members in implementing their own plans for investing in workers.

[53] Hall, Ben, George Parker, and Nikki Tait, European Leaders Decide on Deadline for Reform Blueprint, *Financial Times*, November 8, 2008, p. 7.

[54] *Principles for Sound Stress Testing Practices and Supervision*: Consultative Document, Bank for International Settlements, January 2009.

[55] Munoz, Sara Schaefer, and Alistair MacDonald, U.K. Weighs "Bad Banks," *The Wall Street Journal Europe*, February 4, 2009, p. 2.

[56] Perry, Joellen, and Marcus Walker, Central Bank Mulls "Bad Banks," *The Wall Street Journal Europe*, February 2, 2009, p. 19

[57] CRS Report RS22850, *Tax Provisions of the 2008 Economic Stimulus Package*, coordinated by Jane G. Gravelle.

[58] Dougherty, Carter, British Central Bank Cuts Its Key Rate, *The New York Times*, March 6, 2009*; March 5, 2009 – Monetary Policy Decisions*, press release, the European Central Bank.

[59] *A European Economic Recovery Plan*: Communication From the Commission to the European Council, Commission of the European Communities, COM(2008) 800 final, November 26, 2008. The full report is available at: http://ec.europa.eu/commission_barroso/ president/pdf/ Comm_20081126.pdf

[60] Benoit, Bernard, Germany Doubles Size of Stimulus, *Financial Times*, January 6, 2009, p. 10; Walker, Marcus, Germany's Big Spending Plans, *The Wall Street Journal Europe*, January 13, 2009, p. 3.

[61] Benoit, Bernard, German Stimulus Offers Job Promise, *Financial Times*, December 16, 2008. p. 1.

[62] Walker, Marcus, Germany Mulls $135 Billion in Rescue Loans, *The Wall Street Journal Europe*, January 8, 2009. p. 1.

[63] Benoit, Bernard, A Measured Merkel, *Financial Times*, November 25, 2008, p. 9.

[64] Steinbruck, Peer, Germany's Way Out of the Crisis, *The Wall Street Journal*, December 22, 2008.

[65] Parussini, Gabrielle, France to Give Banks Capital, With More Strings Attached, *The Wall Street Journal Europe*, January 16, 2009, p. A17.

[66] Gauthier-Villars, David, Leading News: France Sets Stimulus Plan, *The Wall Street Journal Europe*, December 5, 2008, p. 3.

[67] Hall, Ben, France Gives Renault and Peugeot E.U.R 779m, *Financial Times*, December 16, 2008, p. 4.

[68] Abboud, Leila, France Considers New Measures to Aid Auto Companies, *The Wall Street Journal Europe*, January 15, 2009, p. 4.

[69] Scott, Mark, Is Britain's Stimulus Plan a Wise Move? *Business Week*, November 24, 2008; Werdigier, Julia, Britain Offers $30 Billion Stimulus Plan, *The New York Times*, November 25, 2008.

[70] Falloon, Matt, and Mike Peacock, UK Government to Borrow Record Sums to Revive Economy, *The Washington Post*, November 24, 2008.

[71] *Real Help for Business*, press release, Department for Business, Enterprise and Regulatory Reform, January 14, 2009; Mollenkamp, Carrick, Alistair MacDonald, and Sara Schaefer Munoz, Hurdles rise as U.K. Widens Stimulus Plan, *The Wall Street Journal Europe*, January 14, 2009, p. 1.

[72] Watt, Nicholas, British Ambassador Responds to German Economic Criticism, *Guardian*, December 12, 2008.

[73] Parker, George, Brown Suffers as Pound Slides, *Financial Times*, December 16, 2008, p. 9.

[74] *OECD Economic Surveys: Europe*, January 2009, Organization for Economic Cooperation and Development, p. 47

[75] Benoit, Bertrand, Tom Braithwaaite, Jimmy Burns, Jean Eaglesham, et. al., Iceland and UK clash on Crisis, Financial Times, October 10, 2008, p. 1.

[76] Evans, Kelly, John W. Milner, and Mei Fong, Trade Decline Adds to the Global Slowdown – Major Nations Post Big Export Retreats as Demand Falls Off, *The Wall Street Journal Europe*, January 14, 2009, p. 2; Lyons, John, Trade- Finance Squeeze Hurts the Healthy, *The Wall Street Journal Europe*, December 22, 2008, p. 10.

[77] Members of the euro area are: Austria, Belgium, Cyprus, Finland, France, Germany, Greece, Ireland, Italy, Luxembourg, Malta, the Netherlands, Portugal, Slovakia, Slovenia, and Spain.

[78] Davies, Ryan J., *MiFID and a Changing Competitive Landscape*, July 2008., p. 3. Available online at: http://faculty.babson.edu/rdavies/MiFID_July2008_Davies15.pdf

[79] *The EU Financial Services Action Plan: A Guide*, HM Treasury, the Financial Services Authority, and the Bank of England, July 31, 2003.

[80] Basel II is the second of the Basel Accords, which are recommendations on banking laws and regulations issued by the Basel Committee on Banking Supervision. The purpose of Basel II is to create an international standard that banking regulators can use when creating regulations concerning requirements for capital adequacy that banks must meet to guard against the types of financial and operational risks that banks face.

In: The Financial Crisis and the European Union ISBN: 978-1-60741-987-7
Editor: Klaus G. Efenhoff

Chapter 4

THE GLOBAL FINANCIAL CRISIS: THE ROLE OF THE INTERNATIONAL MONETARY FUND (IMF)*

Martin A. Weiss†

ABSTRACT

This chapter discusses two potential roles the International Monetary Fund (IMF) may have in helping to resolve the current global financial crisis: (1) immediate crisis control through balance of payments lending to emerging market and less-developed countries and (2) increased surveillance of the global economy through better coordination with the international financial regulatory agencies.

The current global financial crisis, which began with the downturn of the U.S. subprime housing market in 2007, is testing the ability of the International Monetary Fund (IMF), in its role as the central international institution for oversight of the global monetary system. Though the IMF is unlikely to lend to the developed countries most affected by the crisis and must compete with other international financial institutions [1] as a source of ideas and global

---

* This is an edited, reformatted and augmented version of a Congressional Research Service publication, dated February 4, 2009.

† mweiss@crs.loc.gov, 7-5407

macroeconomic policy coordination, the spillover effects of the crisis on emerging and less- developed economies gives the IMF an opportunity to reassert its role in the international economy on two key dimensions of the global financial crisis: (1) immediate crisis management and (2) long-term systemic reform of the international financial system.

The role of the IMF has changed significantly since its founding in July 1944. Late in World War II, delegates from 44 nations gathered in Bretton Woods, New Hampshire to discuss the postwar recovery of Europe and create a set of international institutions to resolve many of the economic issues—such as protectionist trade policies and unstable exchange rates—that had ravaged the international economy between the two world wars. As the global financial system has evolved over the decades, so has the IMF. From 1946 to 1973, the main purpose of the IMF was to manage the fixed system of international exchange rates agreed on at Bretton Woods. The U.S. dollar was fixed to gold at $35 per ounce and all other member countries' currencies were fixed to the dollar at different rates. The IMF monitored the macroeconomic and exchange rate policies of member countries and helped countries overcome balance of payments crises with short-term loans that helped bring currencies back in line with their determined value. This system came to an abrupt end in 1973 when the United States floated its currency and subsequently introduced the modern system of floating exchange rates. Over the past three decades, floating exchange rates and financial globalization have contributed to, in addition to substantial wealth and high levels of growth for many countries, an international economy marred by exchange rate volatility and semi-frequent financial crises. The IMF adapted to the end of the fixed-exchange rate system by becoming the lender of last resort for countries afflicted by such crises.

Current IMF operations and responsibilities can be grouped into three areas: surveillance, lending, and technical assistance. Surveillance involves monitoring economic and financial developments and providing policy advice to member countries. Lending entails the provision of financial resources under specified conditions to assist a country experiencing balance of payments difficulties. Technical assistance includes help on designing or improving the quality and effectiveness of domestic policy-making.

WHITHER THE IMF?

The current financial crisis represents a major challenge for the IMF since the institution is not in financial position to be able to lend to the United States or other Western countries affected by the crisis (with the possible exception of Iceland). The IMF's total financial resources as of August 2008 were $352 billion, of which $257 billion were usable resources [2]. The most the IMF ever lent in any one year period (the four quarters through September 1998 at the height of the Asian financial crisis) was $30 billion. The most lent during any two-year period was $40 billion between June 2001-2003 during the financial crises in Argentina, Brazil, Uruguay, and Turkey [3]. The IMF is wholly unequipped to provide by itself the necessary liquidity to the United States and affected industrialized countries. In addition, the United States and other Western countries, along with some Middle Eastern oil states, are the primary contributors to IMF resources, and it is unlikely that these countries would seek IMF assistance. The last time that developed countries borrowed from the IMF was between1976 and1978, when the United Kingdom, Italy, and Spain borrowed from the IMF to deal with the aftershocks of the 1973 increase in oil prices [4].

Since the financial crises of a decade ago, many emerging market economies, largely in response to their criticism of the policy conditions that the IMF required of countries receiving IMF loans, have built up extensive foreign reserve positions in order to avoid having to return to the IMF should such a crisis occur again [5]. From a level of around $1.2 trillion in 1995, global foreign exchange reserves now exceed $7 trillion. The IMF tabulates that by the second quarter of 2008, developing countries' foreign reserves were $5.47 trillion compared to $1.43 trillion in the industrialized countries [6]. This reserve accumulation was driven by increasing commodity prices (such as oil and minerals) and large current account surpluses combined with high savings rates in emerging Asian countries [7].

Emerging market foreign reserve accumulation fueled by rising commodity prices and large emerging market trade surpluses, and net foreign direct investment flows has led to a decrease in demand for IMF lending and a weakening in the IMF's budget position. IMF lending peaked in 2003 with IMF credit outstanding totaling $110.29 billion. By September 30, 2008, outstanding IMF loans had decreased by $92.6 billion to $17.72 billion (see also figure 1) [8].

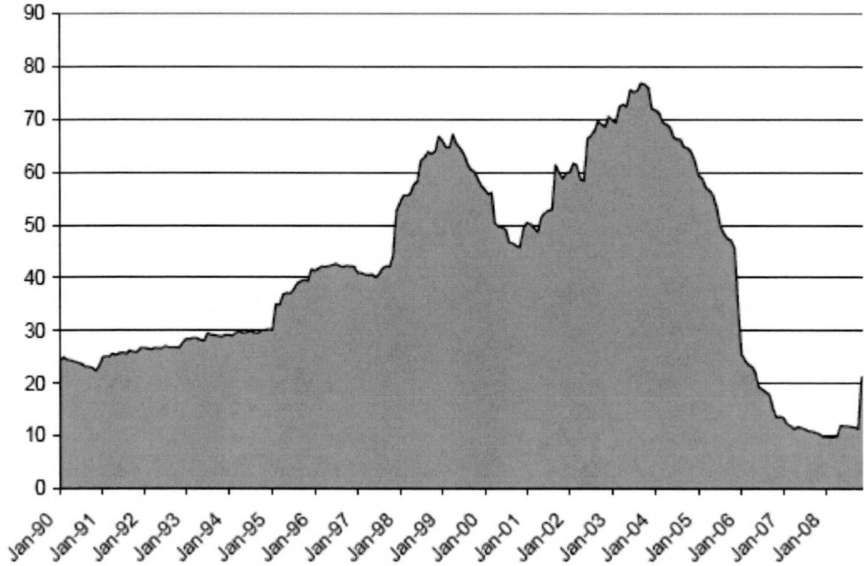

Source: International Monetary Fund.

Notes: The Special Drawing Right (SDR) is an international reserve asset, created by the IMF in 1969. SDRs are allocated to member countries in proportion to their IMF quotas. The SDR also serves as the unit of account of the IMF and some other international organizations. Its value is based on a basket of key international currencies (the U.S. dollar, Euro, Japanese yen, and pound sterling). The SDR currency value is calculated daily and the valuation basket is reviewed and adjusted every five years.

Figure 1. Outstanding IMF Credit (1990–2008, SDR).

Since the IMF earns income on the interest paid on its loans, the decrease in demand for IMF's lending led to a budget shortfall in 2007. The IMF is in the process of seeking authorization from national legislatures to sell a portion of gold that the IMF holds in reserve to create an investment fund whose profits can be used to finance IMF operations and delink IMF operations (such as its global surveillance programs) from profit earned on IMF lending. Congress is expected to face a vote in FY2009 on whether or not to authorize this proposal.

The rise of emerging market countries over the past decade, has created new challenges for the IMF. Many emerging market economies argue that their current stake in the IMF does not represent their role in the world economy. Several countries, particularly in East Asia and South America, believe that their new economic weight and status should afford them a larger quota and a greater voice at the institution. In addition, many poor countries believe that the IMF's quota system is prejudiced against them, giving them little voice even though they are the majority of the IMF's borrowers. In response to these concerns, the IMF embarked in 2006 on a reform process to increase the quota and voice of its emerging market country members [9].

While the IMF has struggled to define its role in the global economy, the global financial crisis has created an opportunity for the IMF to reinvigorate itself and possibly play a constructive role in resolving, or at the least mitigating, the effects of the global downturn, on two fronts: (1) through immediate crisis management, primarily balance of payments support to emerging- market and less-developed countries, and (2) contributing to long-term systemic reform of the international financial system.

Immediate Crisis Management

IMF rules stipulate that countries are allowed to borrow up to three times their quota over a three- year period, although this requirement has been breached on several occasions where the IMF has lent at much higher multiples of quota [10]. While many emerging market countries, such as Brazil, India, Indonesia, and Mexico, have stronger macroeconomic fundamentals than they did a decade ago, a sustained decrease in U.S. imports resulting from an economic slowdown could have recessionary effects overseas. Emerging markets with less robust financial structures have been more dramatically affected, especially those dependent on exports to the United States. Increased emerging market default risk can be seen in the dramatic rise of credit default swap (CDS) prices for emerging market sovereign bonds. Financial markets are currently pricing the risk that Pakistan, Argentina, Ukraine, and Iceland will default on their sovereign debt at above 80% [11]. On October 26, the IMF announced a $16.5 billion agreement with Ukraine. On October 27, the IMF announced a $15.7 billion loan to Hungary. On November 19, the IMF announced a $2.1 billion loan to Iceland. On November 24, the IMF announced a $7.6 billion loan to Pakistan [12]. On December 23, 2008, the IMF announced a $2.35 billion dollar loan for Latvia. Other potential candidates for IMF loans are Serbia, Kazakhstan, Lithuania, and Estonia [13].

IMF Managing Director Dominique Strauss-Kahn has stressed that the IMF is able and poised to assist with crisis loans. At the IMF annual meetings in October 2008, Managing Director Strauss-Kahn announced that the IMF had activated its Emergency Financing Mechanism (EFM) to speed the normal process for loans to crisis-afflicted countries [14]. The emergency mechanism enables rapid approval (usually within 48-72 hours) of IMF lending once an agreement has been reached between the IMF and the national government. As noted before, while normal IMF rules are that countries can only borrow three times the size of their respective quotas over three years, the Fund has shown the willingness in the past to lend higher amounts should the crisis require extraordinary amounts of assistance.

A second instrument that the IMF could use to provide financial assistance is its Exogenous Shock Facility (ESF). The ESF provides policy support and financial assistance to low-income countries facing *exogenous shocks*, events that are completely out of the national government's control. These could include commodity price changes (including oil and food), natural disasters, and conflicts and crises in neighboring countries that disrupt trade. The ESF was modified in 2008 to further increase the speed and flexibility of the IMF's response. Through the ESF, a country can immediately access up to 25% of its quota for each exogenous shock and an additional 75% of quota in phased disbursements over one to two years.

On October 29, 2008, the IMF announced that it plans on creating a new three month short-term lending facility aimed at middle income countries such as Mexico, South Korea, and Brazil. The IMF plans to set aside $100 billion for the new Short-Term Liquidity Facility (SLF). In a unprecedented departure from other IMF programs, SLF loans will have no policy conditionality [15]. Under the SLF, countries with track records of sound policies, access to capital markets and sustainable debt burden can draw up to five times their IMF quota for three months and up to two additional three-month periods. To date, no country has drawn on the SLF. For many middle-income countries this is likely due to the associated stigma of accepting IMF assistance. Concerns have also been raised that by creating a new lending mechanism the IMF is dividing potential borrowers into those that qualify for the SLF and those that would be forced to accept regular IMF lending with its associated policy conditionality [16]. To counter this stigma, some analysts have proposed coordinating an SLF package for several countries at the same time. Another option may be to coordinate an SLF loan with the newly created Federal Reserve swap arrangements for developing countries. On the same day that the IMF announced the SLF, the U.S. Federal Reserve approved $30 billion in reciprocal swap arrangements with four emerging- market countries: Brazil, Korea, Mexico, and Singapore.

At the 2009 Davos World Economic Forum, John Lipsky, the IMF's First Deputy Managing Director, said that to be able to effectively lend to all the potential countries affected by the crisis, the IMF should double its lending resources to around $500 billion [17]. In addition to potential resources freed up by the sale of IMF gold reserves, two additional financing options for the IMF are seeking additional capital from its member countries and selling bonds. The government of Japan has agreed to lend the IMF $100 billion dollars and it is reported that the agreement is almost finalized [18]. According to Mr. Lipsky, the Japanese loan would be structured in a way that is similar to two IMF programs: the General Arrangements to Borrow (GAB) and the New Arrangements to Borrow (NAB), which provide up to $50 billion in additional funding if the IMF were to exceed that amount available in its core resources. The second option would be for the IMF to issue bonds, which it has never done in its 60 year history. According to Mr. Lipsky, the IMF bonds would be sold to central banks and government agencies. According to economist and former IMF chief economist Michael Mussa, the United States and Europe blocked attempts by the IMF to issue bonds since it could potentially make the IMF less dependent on them for financial resources and thus less willing to take policy direction from them [19]. However, several other multilateral institutions such as the World Bank and the regional development banks routinely issue bonds to help finance their lending.

The IMF is not alone in making available financial assistance to crisis-afflicted countries. The International Finance Corporation (IFC), the private-sector lending arm of the World Bank, has announced that it will launch a $3 billion fund to capitalize small banks in poor countries that are battered by the financial crisis. The Inter-American Development Bank (IDB) announced on October 10, 2008 that it will offer a new $6 billion credit line to member governments, as well as increase its more traditional lending for specific projects [20]. In addition to the IDB, the Andean Development Corporation (CAF) announced a liquidity facility of $1.5 billion and the Latin American Fund of Reserves (FLAR) has offered to make available $4.5 billion in contingency lines. While these amounts may be insufficient should Brazil, Argentina, or any other large Latin American country need a rescue package, they could be very helpful for smaller countries such as those in the Caribbean and Central America that are heavily dependent on tourism and property investments [21].

In Asia, where countries were left no choice but to accept IMF rescue packages a decade ago, efforts are under way to promote regional financial cooperation, so that governments can avoid having to borrow from the IMF in a financial crisis. One result of these efforts is the Chiang Mai Initiative, a network of bilateral swap arrangements among east and Southeast Asian countries. In addition, Japan, South Korea, and China have backed the creation of a $10 billion crisis fund. Contributions are expected from bilateral donors, the Asian Development Bank (ADB), and the World Bank [22].

Lastly, economic conditions over the past decade have created a new class of bilateral creditors who could challenge the IMF's role as the lender of last resort. The rise of oil prices has created vast wealth among Middle Eastern countries and persistent trade surpluses in Asia have created a new class of emerging creditors. These countries either have the foreign reserves to support their own currencies in a financial crisis, or they are a potential source of loans for other countries.

REFORMING GLOBAL MACROECONOMIC SURVEILLANCE

In addition to revising its emergency lending assistance guidelines to make the IMF's financial assistance more attractive to potential borrowers, there is a role for the IMF to play in the broader reform of the global financial system. Efforts are underway to expand the IMF's ability to conduct effective multilateral surveillance of the international economy. In addition, there are efforts to increase cooperation with the international financial standard setters as the Financial Stability Forum (FSF), the Bank for International Settlements (BIS), as well as in various international working groups such as the Basel Committee on Banking Supervision and the Joint Forum on Risk Assessment and Capital. The deepening interconnectedness of the international economy may call for such increased cooperation between the IMF, which performs global macroeconomic surveillance, and the individual global financial regulatory bodies.

The IMF Articles of Agreement require (Article IV) that the IMF "oversee the international monetary system in order to ensure its effective operation" and to "oversee the compliance of each member with its obligations" to the Fund. In particular, "the Fund shall exercise firm surveillance over the exchange rate policies of member countries and shall adopt specific principles for the guidance of all members with respect to those policies." Countries are required to provide the IMF with information and to consult with the IMF upon its request. The IMF staff generally meets each year with each member country for "Article IV consultations" regarding the country's current fiscal and monetary policies, the state of its economy, its exchange rate situation, and other relevant concerns. The IMF's reports on its annual Article IV consultations with each country are presented to the IMF executive board along with the staff's observations and recommendations about possible improvements in the country's economic policies and practices.

As the global financial system has become increasingly interconnected, the IMF has conducted multilateral surveillance beyond two bi-annual reports it produces, the *World Economic Outlook* and the *Global Financial Stability Report,* four regional reports, and regular IMF contributions to intergovernmental fora and committees, including the Group of Seven and Group of Twenty, and the Financial Stability Forum. These efforts at multilateral surveillance, however, have been criticized as being less than fully effective, too focused on bilateral issues, and not fully accounting for the risks of contagion that have been seen in the current crisis. A 2006 report by the IMF's internal watchdog agency, the Independent Evaluation Office (IEO) found that, "multilateral surveillance has not sufficiently explored options to deal with policy spillovers in a global context; the language of multilateral advice is no more based on explicit consideration of economic linkages and policy spillovers than that of bilateral advice."[23] Participants at an October 2008 IMF panel on the future of the IMF reiterated these concerns, adding that many developed countries have impeded the IMF's efforts at multilateral surveillance by largely ignoring IMF's bilateral surveillance of their own economies and not fully embracing the IMF's first attempt at multilateral consultations on global imbalances in 2006. According to Trevor Manuel, South Africa's Finance Minister, "one has to start from the fundamental view that if you accept public policy and you accept the interconnectedness of the global economy, then you need an institution appropriate to its regulation."[24] Analysts argue, however, that developed countries have long ignored IMF advice on their economic policy, while at the same time pressuring the IMF to use its role in patrolling the exchange rate system to support their own foreign economic goals.

REFERENCES

[1] Such as the Bank for International Settlements, Financial Stability Forum (FSF), and the Organization for Economic Cooperation and Development (OECD).

[2] IMF resources that are considered non-usable to finance IMF operations are (1) its gold holdings, (2) the currencies of members that are using IMF resources and are therefore, by definition, in a weak balance of payments or reserve position, (3) the currencies of other members with relatively weak external positions, and (4) other non-liquid IMF assets.

[3] Brad Setser, "Extraordinary Times," Council on Foreign Relations, September 29, 2008. It is worth noting that the final rescue packages during the Asian crisis totaled many times $30 billion once bilateral assistance was included.

[4] Oxford Analytica, "IMF reaffirms role in global economy." October 15, 2008.

[5] Many analysts believe that the tight monetary and fiscal policies that the IMF required of countries accepting IMF loans accentuated the immediate economic impact of the crisis while having marginal impact on the countries' longterm structural reform.

[6] IMF Currency Composition of Official Foreign Exchange Reserves (COFER) available at http://www.imf.org/external/np/sta/cofer/eng/index.htm.

[7] Georges Pineau and Ettore Dorruci, "The Accumulation of Foreign Reserves," *European Central Bank*, March 2006.

[8] Total IMF Credit Outstanding for all members from 1984-2008, available at http://www.imf.org/external/np/fin/tad/extcred1.aspx.

[9] For background, see CRS Report RL33626, *International Monetary Fund: Reforming Country Representation*, by Martin A. Weiss

[10] The 1997 package for South Korea was 19 times as large as their quota at the IMF.

[11] David Oakley, "Emerging Nations hit by growing debt fears," *Financial Times*, October 14, 2008.

[12] Information on ongoing IMF negotiations is available at http://www.imf.org.

[13] Oxford Analytica, "IMF reaffirms role in the global economy." October 15, 2008.

[14] The EFM was set up in 1995 and has been used on six occasions—in 1997 for the Philippines, Thailand, Indonesia, and Korea; in 2001 for Turkey; and in 2008 for Georgia.

[15] "IMF to Launch New Facility for Emerging Markets Hit by Crisis," *IMF Survey Online*, October 29, 2008.

[16] Edwin Truman, On What Terms is the IMF Worth Funding, *Peterson Institute for International Economics*, December 2008.

[17] "As Contingency, IMF Aims to Double its Lendable Resources," *IMF Survey Magazine: Policy*, February 2, 2008.

[18] "IMF talks to borrow $100 billion from Japan almost completed," *Japan Times*, February 4, 2009.

[19] Bob Davis, "IMF Considers Issuing Bonds to Raise Money," *Wall Street Journal*, February 1, 2009

[20] Bob Davis, "International Groups Offer Latin America More Loans," *Wall Street Journal*, October 14, 2008.

[21] "Q&A: Central American "Exports, Production, Employment" Hit by Crisis" *Inter Press Service News Agency*, October 14, 2008.

[22] Malcolm Moore, "Asia Mounts its own Bank Bailout," *The Daily Telegraph*, October 15, 2008.

[23] Independent Evaluation Office (IEO) of the IMF, *An Evaluation of the IMF's Multilateral Surveillance*, September 1, 2006.

[24] Camilla Anderson, "Future Role of IMF Debated As Financial Crisis Takes Toll," *IMF Survey Online*, October 16, 2008.

In: The Financial Crisis and the European Union
Editor: Klaus G. Efenhoff
ISBN: 978-1-60741-987-7

Chapter 5

ICELAND'S FINANCIAL CRISIS*

James K. Jackson

ABSTRACT

On November 19, 2008, Iceland and the International Monetary Fund (IMF) finalized an agreement on a $6 billion economic stabilization program supported by a $2.1 billion loan from the IMF. Following the IMF decision, Denmark, Finland, Norway, and Sweden agreed to provide an additional $2.5 billion. Iceland's banking system had collapsed as a culmination of a series of decisions the banks made that left them highly exposed to disruptions in financial markets. The collapse of the banks also raises questions for U.S. leaders and others about supervising banks that operate across national borders, especially as it becomes increasingly difficult to distinguish the limits of domestic financial markets. Such supervision is important for banks that are headquartered in small economies, but operate across national borders. If such banks become so overexposed in foreign markets that a financial disruption threatens the solvency of the banks, the collapse of the banks can overwhelm domestic credit markets and outstrip the ability of the central bank to serve as the lender of last resort.

* This is an edited, reformatted and augmented version of a Congressional Research Service publication, **dated November 20, 2008.**

BACKGROUND

Iceland [1] is the smallest economy within the Organization for Economic Cooperation and Development (OECD) with a gross domestic product (GDP) in 2007 of about $11.8 billion, as indicated in table 1. Historically, Iceland's economy has been based on marine and energy resources. More recently, Iceland has developed a strong services sector, which accounts for two-thirds of the economic output. Since 2000, Iceland has experienced particularly strong growth in its financial services sector. Trade accounts for a large share of Iceland's GDP, with imports and exports of goods and services equivalent in value to 46% and 35%, respectively, of GDP. Fish and other marine products were Iceland's main export item until 2006, when Iceland began to capitalize on its abundant thermal energy resources to produce and export aluminum. As the data in table 1 indicate, Iceland is expected to experience a slowdown in its rate of economic growth in 2008 and is projected by the International Monetary Fund to experience a negative rate of growth in 2009. Iceland also has battled a high and rising rate of inflation, as measured by the consumer price index (CPI) and interest rates, as measured by the long-term government bond rates.

Table 1. Iceland: Main Economic Indicators and Projections (in billions of dollars and in percent)

	2004	2005	2006	2007	2008	2009
		Actual			Projected	
GDP (in $billions)	$9.9	$10.6	$11.1	$11.8	NA	NA
Real GDP growth	7.7%	7.4%	4.4%	4.9%	0.3%	–3.1%
CPI	3.2%	4.0%	6.8%	5.0%	12.1%	11.2%
Interest rates	7.5%	7.7%	9.3%	9.8%	11.4%	10.3%

Source: *World Economic Outlook*, October 2008, International Monetary Fund; and *Economic Outlook*, Preliminary Edition, June 2008, Organization for Economic Cooperation and Development.

RECENT ECONOMIC ACTIVITY

A combination of economic factors over the early to mid-2000s led to Iceland's current economic and banking distress. In particular, access to easy credit, a boom in domestic construction that fueled rapid economic growth, and a broad deregulation of Iceland's financial sector spurred the banks to expand rapidly abroad and eventually played a role in the eventual financial collapse. Iceland benefitted from favorable global financial conditions that reduced the cost of credit and a sweeping liberalization of its domestic financial sector that spurred rapid growth and encouraged Iceland's banks to spread quickly throughout Europe.

In 2004, Iceland's commercial banks increased their activity in the country's mortgage market by competing directly with the state-run Housing Financing Fund (HFF), which had been the major provider of mortgage loans. In contrast to the Housing Financing Fund, the commercial banks began offering loans with lower interest rates, longer maturities, and a higher loan to value ratio. Also, the banks did not require a real estate purchase as a precondition for a loan, which made it possible for homeowners to refinance existing mortgages and to access the equity in their homes for consumption or investment purposes. These measures spurred an expansion in credit and caused real estate prices to soar. In addition, the improving economic conditions led to an expansion in consumer spending which resulted in rising inflation and a larger trade deficit. As a further stimulus to the economy, the Icelandic government reduced both direct and indirect taxes, which provided further impetus to consumer spending.

By 2004, Iceland's central bank began tightening monetary policy by raising interest rates in an attempt to curtail inflationary pressures. Between 2004 and 2007, the Bank raised nominal short-term interest rates from 5% to 15%. The increase in interest rates, however, was not reflected in the interest rates the Housing Financing Fund charged for mortgages. As a result, the comparatively low interest rates charged by the HFF pushed up demand for housing which, in turn, further inflated the price of homes in Iceland. In addition, since the commercial banks were willing to make loans based on the equity in a home, the rising equity values in housing allowed consumers to finance a higher level of consumption, with the attendant pressure on inflation and interest rates. At the same time, the higher domestic interest rates made bond issues in krona attractive to foreign investors who could borrow abroad at low interest rates, which placed upward pressure on the value of the krona and worsened the trade deficit.

As Iceland deregulated its commercial banks, those banks expanded to the United Kingdom, the United States, Scandinavia, continental Europe, and elsewhere. Iceland has five commercial banks: Glitnir, Kaupthing, Nyi Landsbanki, Straumur Investment Bank, and Icebank, which serves as the clearing house for the 20 locally-run savings banks. The three largest banks, Kaupthing, Landsbanki, and Glitnir, have total assets of more than $168 billion, or 14 times

Iceland's GDP. Iceland also has 20 savings banks, with assets at the end of 2007 valued at $9 billion.

After Iceland deregulated its commercial banks, the banks expanded their operations abroad by acquiring subsidiaries in commercial banking and in securities brokerages. At the end of 2007, almost half of the total assets of the largest commercial banking groups were accounted for by foreign subsidiaries, most of them located in Northern Europe, and in 2007 about 58% of their overall income was generated from their subsidiaries located abroad. By the end of 2007, Iceland's three largest banks relied on short-term financing for 75% of their funds, mostly through borrowing in the money markets and in the short-term interbank market. Iceland's banks are a hybrid between commercial and investment banks, with relatively large exposure to market risk. By March 2008, investors had become wary of Iceland's banks due to their large funding needs and high dependence on short-term funds in money markets. Even before the financial crisis erupted in fall 2008, the Central Bank of Iceland and other institutions forecasted a slowdown or a contraction in Iceland's rate of economic growth in 2008 and 2009.

BANKING COLLAPSE

Between October 7 and 9, 2008, Iceland's Financial Supervisory Authority (FSA), an independent state authority with responsibilities to regulate and supervise Iceland's credit, insurance, securities, and pension markets, took control of, without actually nationalizing them, three of Iceland's largest banks: Landsbanki, Glitnir Banki, and Kaupthing Bank. The takeover occurred prior to a scheduled vote by shareholders to accept a government plan to purchase the shares of the banks in order to head off the collapse of the banks. At the same time, Iceland suspended trading on its stock exchange for two days [2].

The takeover of the banks was orchestrated in an attempt to quell a sharp depreciation in the exchange value of the Icelandic krona. The krona depreciated relative to the euro and the dollar between January 2008 and July 2008; the depreciation became more pronounced after July 2008. For Iceland, which relies heavily on trade, a sharp depreciation in its currency increases the costs of its imports and adds to domestic inflationary pressures.

The demise of Iceland's three largest banks is attributed to an array of events, but primarily stems from decisions by the banks themselves. Some observers argued that the collapse of Lehman Brothers set in motion the events that finally led to the collapse of the banks [3], but this conclusion is controversial. Some have argued that at the heart of Iceland's banking crisis is a flawed banking model that is based on an internationally active banking sector that is large relative to the size of the home country's GDP and to the fiscal capacity of the central bank [4]. As a result, a disruption in liquidity threatens the viability of the banks and overwhelms the ability of the central bank to act as the lender of last resort, which undermines the solvency of the banking system.

By the time of the acknowledged start of the global financial crisis in mid-2007, Iceland's central bank and Iceland's banks themselves had begun to recognize the vulnerability of the banks. In particular, officials in Iceland as well as financial observers in Europe had begun to reassess the risks associated with various financial instruments, and to raise questions about the asset strength of the banks and the asset size of the banks relative to the size of Iceland's economy. In addition, by late 2007, various organizations had begun to recognize the imbalances that were becoming apparent in Iceland's economy and had forecast a slowdown in Iceland's torrid pace of economic growth for 2008 and 2009 [5].

When Lehman Brothers collapsed, the international financial markets had already begun to reassess the risks associated with a broad range of financial instruments. Eventually, this reassessment of risks undermined the remaining amount of trust that existed in the credit markets, which caused banks and other financial firms to grow unwilling to make loans to short-term money markets and to engage in interbank lending, which caused those activities to freeze up. For Iceland's three largest banks, this collapse in short-term borrowing meant that they found that it was increasingly difficult to finance debts in the interbank market.

In addition, Iceland's Landsbanki and Kaupthing Bank experienced a sharp rise in the cost of private deposit insurance. This withdrawal of credit eliminated a major source of the bank's funding and threatened their ability to finance the nation's trade deficits. Typically, this situation is remedied by the central bank, which stands as the bank of last resort. In Iceland's case, however, the debts of the commercial banks were so large that Iceland's central bank was unable to guarantee the banks' loans, which lead to the collapse of the banks. In turn, the krona experienced a serious depreciation in its value, which raised the cost of imports and threatened to fuel domestic inflation. The large foreign debts held by Iceland's banks proved to be unsupportable once they could not utilize the interbank market to refinance their substantial loans.

The FSA transferred part of the three banks' operations to new bank entities that it formed and that are fully owned by the Icelandic Government. As part of these actions, the FSA dismissed the members of the boards of directors and appointed individuals to serve on a Receivership Committee. The respective committees assumed supervision of the assets and operations of the newly-formed banks. During the same two-day period, Iceland's central bank abandoned its attempt to maintain the value of the krona. With the take-over of the three major banks, the central bank effectively shut down the last clearing houses for trading krona.

On October 15, 2008, the Central Bank of Iceland set up a temporary system of daily currency auction to facilitate international trade. Without a viable currency, there was no way to support the banks, which have done the bulk of their business in foreign markets. The financial crisis also created problems with Great Britain, because hundreds of thousands of Britons hold accounts in online branches of the Icelandic banks and fear those accounts will all default. The government of British Prime Minister Gordon Brown has used powers granted under anti-terrorism laws to freeze British assets of Landsbanki until the standoff is resolved.

On November 19, 2008, Iceland and the International Monetary Fund (IMF) finalized an agreement on an economic stabilization program supported by a $2.1 billion two-year standby arrangement from the IMF [6]. Upon approval of the IMF's Executive board, the IMF released $827 million immediately to Iceland with the remainder to be paid in eight equal installments, subject to quarterly reviews. As part of the agreement, Iceland has proposed a plan to restore confidence in its banking system, to stabilize the exchange rate, and to improve the nation's fiscal position. Also, as part of the plan, Iceland's central bank raised its key interest rate by six percentage points to 18% on October 29, 2008 to attract foreign investors and to shore up its sagging currency [7]. The IMF's Executive Board had postponed its decision on a loan to Iceland three times, reportedly to give IMF officials more time to confirm loans made by other nations. Other observers argued, however, that the delay reflected objections by British, Dutch, and German officials over the disposition of deposit accounts operated by Icelandic banks in their countries. Iceland reportedly smoothed the way by agreeing in principle to cover the deposits, although the details had not be finalized. In a joint statement, Germany, Britain, and the Netherlands said on November 20, 2008 that they would "work constructively in the continuing discussions" to reach an agreement [8]. Following the decision of IMF's Executive Board, Denmark, Finland, Norway, and Sweden agreed to provide an additional $2.5 billion in loans to Iceland.

CONCLUSIONS

The failure of Iceland's banks raises questions about bank supervision and crisis management for governments in Europe and the United States. This incident raises questions about how national governments should address the issue of supervising foreign financial firms that are operating within their borders and how to protect their depositors when a foreign-owned firm may attempt to withdraw deposits from one market in order to offset losses in another. One approach focuses on broad levels of cooperation between national governments with each government addressing the crisis from its own perspective and in its own limited way. For a number of governments in Europe this approach is appealing, because their economies and their banks have felt little direct effect from the crisis.

An alternative approach argues in favor of a more integrated and coordinated response from national governments and central banks. Proponents of this approach argue that a coordinated systemic approach is necessary, because financial markets in the United States and Europe have become highly integrated as a result of cross-border investment by banks, securities brokers, and other financial firms. As a result of this integration, economic and financial developments that affect national economies are difficult to contain and are quickly transmitted across national borders, as attested to by the financial crisis of 2008. As financial firms react to a financial crisis in one area, their actions can spill over to other areas as they withdraw assets from foreign markets to shore up their domestic operations. For instance, as Icelandic banks began to default, Britain used an anti-terrorism law to seize the deposits of the banks to prevent the banks from shifting funds from Britain to Iceland.[9] Banks and financial firms in Europe have felt the repercussions of the U.S. financial crisis as bank balance sheets have deteriorated and as U.S. firms and European firms have adjusted their operations in response to the crisis.

The Icelandic case also raises questions about the cost and benefits of branch banking across national borders where banks can grow to be so large that disruptions in the financial market can cause defaults that outstrip the resources of national central banks to address. Such branch banking across national borders has significantly expanded financial opportunities for individual investors and firms alike and is unlikely to disappear as a result of the current financial crisis. Nevertheless, if some financial institutions are deemed to be too big to fail, financial regulators and national governments may be called on to address the issue of how such institutions should be supervised when their operations span national borders and they are engaged in a vast array of banking and investment operations.

REFERENCES

[1] This report relies heavily on: *The Economy of Iceland*, The Central Bank of Iceland, August 2008.

[2] Wardell, Jane, Iceland's Financial Crisis Escalates, *Business Week*, October 9, 2008; Pfanner, Eric, Meltdown of Iceland's Financial System Quickens, *The New York Times*, October 9, 2008.

[3] Portes, Richard, The Shocking Errors Behind Iceland's Meltdown, *Financial Times*, October 13, 2008, p. 15.

[4] Buiter, Willem H., and Anne Sibert, *The Icelandic Banking Crisis and What to Do About it: The Lender of Last Resort Theory of Optimal Currency Areas*. Policy Insight No. 26, Centre for Economic Policy Research, October 2008. p. 2.

[5] The Economy of Iceland, p. 9-11.

[6] Anderson, Camilla, Iceland Gets Help to Recover From Historic Crisis, *IMF Survey Magazine*, November 19, 2008.

[7] Iceland Raises Key Rate by 6 Percentage Points, *The New York Times*, October 29, 2008.

[8] Jolly, David, Nordic Countries Add $2.5 Billion to Iceland's Bailout, *The New York Times*, November 20, 2008.

INDEX

A

B

C

D

E

F

G

H

I

J

K

L

M

Q

R

S

T

U

V

W

Y

Z